THE DELIGHT OF MY HEART

-A Mother's Journey Through Grief-

"To do Your will, O my God, is my delight..."
Psalm 40:9

Christine Alfaro

ISBN: 9781793032102
Imprint: Independently published

Dedicated to my husband, Chris, for his steadfast faith and love,

and to our children:
Michael & Meg, Andrea, Seth, Ethan, Caleb, Mary, and Peter

and grandchildren:
Christopher, David, Brandon and all those yet to come...

"...Take care and be earnestly on your guard not to forget the things which your own eyes have seen, nor let them slip from your memory as long as you live, but teach them to your children and to your children's children" (Deuteronomy 4:9).

PRAYERS OF A BROKEN HEART

Dear Lord,

I buried John David three months ago - and with him I feel I've buried a huge part of myself. I feel dead inside. I feel so broken and only sadness in the numbness. I feel so trapped inside - so alone - it's like I've buried all that I feel and like I'll never feel [alive] again. I already had a problem with showing joy and making myself vulnerable in that way. Now it's just getting worse and worse. You keep crushing my joy. I feel like You're stomping the life right out of me. I know in my head that You are not trying to hurt me - but it does hurt! I know there must be something You can teach me in all this - but I hate it. I'm so afraid that I won't come through this - that I'll be lost forever. I hate who I am right now, but I feel powerless to change it. I know that You can change it, not me, but it is hard to seek You. I feel like You've allowed all this and then abandoned me. Maybe it's me who abandoned You - but it's hard to come to You for comfort - knowing that You didn't have to let this happen. You could have changed it all - I wanted You to - I begged You to, and I believed - I trusted that You would heal my baby - but You didn't. Why not? ... Why did You lead me to believe in the miracle, knowing that You weren't going to do it? You smashed my hope and my joy once again. How much must I bear? How long will You continue to tear apart my heart and stomp on my joy? I know You are trying to help me and teach me, but that doesn't make me feel any better. In fact, it makes me feel worse, because then I feel like it's wrong to be mad and hurt. I hate that I can't understand. I hate that I have to try to live divinely, when I am only human and can't possibly even begin to understand.

I want to be a woman of joy - but I'm not. I've become a cold, numb, dead person inside. I hate the kind of wife and mother I've become. I want to feel. I want to be true to myself and others. I want to be alive. I want joy. I'm so sick of feeling this way - of not feeling and not expressing. I want to laugh even if no one else does. I want a smile to be my normal. I want to cry and cry and cry and release all the death within me.

I know I need You - but the thought of making up with You is so hard to bear - because I feel so hurt by You - so mad. Where are You? I don't feel You anymore. I just feel sadness and so so so alone. You hurt me. You led me with false joy and hope for two months, knowing full well how crushed I was going to be. I know You didn't try to crush me - that it's all for good - but that doesn't take away the pain and how I feel. I hurt. I'm so hurt by You. Where are You? I'm left alone now - I don't want to die inside, but I feel like I am. I'm afraid to be this way. I'm afraid it won't ever change. I'm afraid of who I've become - I hate it!

Sometimes when I hold the kids, I feel cold and withdrawn and like I'm an empty vessel holding them - like I'm not even there. I feel so alone, so withdrawn. I feel like I'm lost, and I'm afraid that I will be lost forever. I don't want to be this way. But even when I feel like I'm doing this to the kids, I still can't find my heart and give it to them. This scares me. It's got to affect them. I don't want to hurt them. I want to feel them and them to feel me.

Even though I am angry and hurt, please come to me. I know I need You. Don't leave me alone. Don't abandon me, and don't let me abandon You. I need You. I want to feel Your presence. I need to feel Your presence. I don't want to be alone, and I don't want the children to be *alone without me. Please help me. Mend my broken heart. Help me to feel and experience the joys and pains of this life and be true to them and live and feel through them ... Pull me back to You. Please embrace me, and let me feel Your love. Show Your love to me and bring me back to life again - even more vibrant and alive than before. Heal all the hurts. Make me true to who I am...*

These were the cries of a broken heart, my broken heart: a heart full of grief. A heart that had been shattered three times. My heart was so broken that it hurt too much to feel. My heart became numb and cold. And while I was crying out to God for help, He could not enter because I had closed my heart and could no longer receive His love. I wrote this letter to God, but did not close it. I couldn't, because I was not willing to let go of the anger I felt and surrender to God's will and God's way of loving me.

Each of you reading this has your own story, your own broken heart. You may not feel angry, but you have your own crosses and your own reasons for being hurt, afraid, broken . . . What pain, sorrow, anger, resentment, frustration, fear, worry, or suffering are you unwilling or unable to release and offer to God, trusting His plan for your life? Maybe it's not even suffering holding you back. What dream or desire are you gripping tightly and refusing to entrust to God?

My dream was to be a wife and mother. It was all I wanted. Little did I know the pain and sorrow that could accompany the joy of being a mother. In this book, I will share with you the joys and sorrows that my husband, Chris, and I experienced with the births of our children. I will attempt to walk you through my grief. In each incident you will see some similarities but also many differences. Each event is its own. Hopefully, through the process, you will see the transformation I underwent during my fourth encounter with grief. It came through a surrender of my will to God's. That which I feared ended up filling my life with a new hope and a new joy. It's hard to comprehend that the things we fear the most can be sources of blessing and even joy when we open our hearts fully to God's will and God's love.

Suffering and trials, as we all know, are a very real part of life that none of us can escape. But God has shown me that there is joy in the cross. His will is best, and He will delight us in it, if we let Him. *Surrender* is the key.

Here is my story:

MICHAEL FREDRICK ALFARO
October 9, 1989

Ten short months after our wedding, my husband, Chris, and I were eagerly awaiting the birth of our first child. All I had ever wanted was to be a wife and mother. God granted me my heart's desire on December 17, 1988, just one week after college graduation, when I married my husband. Only twenty-one years old, I became pregnant one month later, which in my mind was one month too long. I was young, eager, and naive, so excited to think that there was a new life inside me, a tiny little human being that would have life for all eternity, even if I miscarried. Ignorant of what pregnancy could do to my emotions, I was not prepared for such intense hormonal changes. I would get super sensitive and cry for no apparent reason or feel down and depressed at times, with no cause. Again, being ignorant of the strength of pregnancy hormones, I just thought I was a pretty bad new wife.

As my due date drew closer, I was bombarded with all the labor and delivery horror stories. Still, I was so excited to experience the joy and miracle of birth. We even had talked about someday in the future maybe trying a home birth. I was super optimistic about it and just so excited. When we arrived at the hospital, even the man escorting us to labor and delivery was excited for us. He said, "this is when you meet God!" I couldn't wait.

As labor progressed, the doctors decided to break my water. Complications arose immediately. Even though I was only dilated to four centimeters, my body began to try to push the baby out. It wasn't an "urge" to push like they had described in childbirth classes. My body was just pushing, whether I wanted it to or not. Everything seemed out of control, and we could no longer hear the baby's heart tones. The doctors quickly tried an internal monitor, but there was still no heartbeat. They rushed me from the ninth floor to the fifth floor for an emergency C-section. Doctors and nurses were literally running my bed through the halls, slamming doors open, and scrambling to get all the necessary people and equipment in place. In the elevator, I looked behind me to my husband stuck in the corner and said, "Don't leave me . . ." The nurse, very abruptly, got right in my face and said he couldn't go with me since it was an emergency. They shoved my bed up to the operating table and yelled at me to get on. I was awake through their prep and heard them say they were ready to begin. The last thing I remember was thinking, "I might not make it through this." I began to pray a Hail Mary, but was asleep long before I could finish the prayer.

A couple of hours later, I woke up alone in a recovery room, not knowing if my baby was dead or alive. Finally, a nurse came in and told me I had a beautiful, healthy baby boy. I just cried when I saw him. It was not exactly the miracle birth I had anticipated. All of our family and friends had already seen him before I did. His birth wasn't peaceful, joyful, or beautiful, but *he* was. So it was nonetheless a miracle and a gift beyond compare. We were parents. Little did I know then the depth of both joy and sorrow I would experience as a mother, and the ways God would stretch and change me through motherhood.

I remember holding this tiny newborn baby, and being overwhelmed with a kind of love I had never known before, a love you can't adequately describe, that no one can fully understand until they experience it. It was an unconditional, all-consuming love for this little person who I didn't even know. I remember looking at our son, Michael, and thinking, "Who are you? I don't even know you, but I love you so much! I would do anything for you." It was overwhelming, unbelievable, and amazing. Though it was a tough delivery, we were immeasurably blessed. We were parents, and our lives were forever changed by our beautiful son, Michael.

Shortly after delivery, my hormones and emotions returned to normal once again. I felt relief, thinking, "Ah, I'm back!" I realized then that all the crazy emotions were from the pregnancy and that maybe I wasn't going to be such a bad, uptight wife after all. I was happy to be my normal self again, and thrilled to be a mother.

Michael brought us a joy and fulfillment we had never known before. He had an adorable smirk and a gentle spirit. He was my little guy, and I loved watching him grow and seeing his little personality come out more and more each day. Other than being sleep-deprived, parenting Michael was a pretty easy road.

TRINIDAD JOSEPH ALFARO

October 8, 1991

When Michael was one, I became pregnant again. Recognizing the hormonal changes that take place in pregnancy, I dealt with my crazy emotions much better this time, but there was one thing I struggled with throughout the pregnancy. I couldn't imagine how I could love another child as much as I loved Michael. I was afraid that loving another baby would take away from my love for him. Because of this, I had a hard time bonding with the baby during my second pregnancy. In fact, I only remember one time having told this little one, "Mommy loves you," during the pregnancy. It bothered me that I felt this way, but I didn't really worry about it. I figured once the baby was born, everything would all make sense. After all, families from the beginning of time have had more than one child and love them all.

The pregnancy went really well, and I was due to have our second child October 31, just a couple of weeks after Michael would turn two. On October 8, however, the day before Michael's second birthday, I was scheduled for my regular OB check-up in the morning. It had been a good pregnancy, and I only had three-and-a-half weeks left until my due date. My niece had just been born on the 5th, and my sister-in-law and I were excited to be having babies at the same time. Life was good, beautiful, full of excitement and great expectation . . .

The night before my doctor appointment, I woke up and became very restless, realizing I couldn't remember when I had last felt the baby move. I had been having constant Braxton Hicks contractions for the past three days and couldn't distinguish between the baby's movements and the Braxton Hicks, which are sort-of practice contractions. Getting out of bed and pacing the floor, I prayed that I would feel the baby move. Time passed, but still no movement. I felt very anxious and could not go back to sleep. Lying restlessly back in bed, I imagined myself delivering a baby who had already died, but then I had a sense of God saying to me, "You can do this." God's peace came over me, and strangely, I was able to fall back to sleep. The next morning when I woke up, I was filled with disbelief over what had happened during the night. I was afraid, and told my husband about it. I really hoped I had just let my mind wander during the night and was actually worrying about nothing.

When we arrived at the doctor's office, however, my fears were confirmed: he could not find the baby's heartbeat. He sent us right over to the hospital for an ultrasound. They told us then that the baby was dead, and that he had probably died about three days earlier. That was most likely the reason for the constant contractions I had been having. Our response was silence - total disbelief. How could this be happening?

Next was a whirlwind of decisions and plans to make. We chose to deliver the baby by C-section. Given the circumstances, I didn't want the labor to go on long and end up having the baby's birthday on the same day as Michael's. I also didn't think that I could emotionally handle labor and delivery under the circumstances. I told the doctor that he could use whatever drugs necessary to keep me under control. Not knowing what to expect and how I would respond, I was so afraid I wouldn't be able to handle the situation and would become hysterical or something. After all, I was only twenty-three years old, and terrified of death. What would death look like? What would it be like to hold my lifeless child? How would I handle it? Could I handle it?

They sent us home to pack our bags and get things together before the surgery later that evening. My husband began making phone calls to notify family and friends. Then the questions began to come about what we would do after the baby's birth. Would we have a funeral? What do you do in this situation? We didn't know. This was all such a shock to us. We could hardly think straight. I only knew of one other woman who had had a stillborn baby, at about four or five months gestation. She had a small, quiet service in the hospital with our parish priest. So we thought maybe that was what should be done in such situations; however, my sister and another close friend urged us to have a full funeral at the church.

Later that day, I delivered my second child. It was an indescribable experience for my husband to see the blue, lifeless baby taken from within me. There was no newborn cry; only silence filled the air. We were told we had another son, whom we named Trinidad Joseph. Trinidad was after Chris's grandfather who had come over to the U.S. from Mexico, and Joseph was after Chris's brother who had died at the age of five months. We had planned on calling him Trini.

After I came out of recovery and was settled in my room, the nurses brought our son, Trini, to us. He was beautifully and lovingly wrapped in newborn baby blankets and had on a little hat. We held and kissed our son for the first and only time. Looking back on the experience, I wish I would have held him longer and opened his little blanket and studied his little baby fingers and toes, but at the time I was so afraid, so numb. I think we just went through the motions and did what we had to do. I guess I didn't know what else I could do. But I know that despite my fear of death, I fell deeply in love with Trini the moment I laid eyes on him. Instantly my worry about how I could love another baby like I loved Michael was gone. My heart overflowed with love for my precious little baby boy, my son, Trini.

The doctors did not know why Trini had died. His autopsy showed that every organ had developed perfectly. We were told that it was just a rare, one-in-a-million occurrence that we should never have to worry about happening again.

We had a beautiful funeral for Trini with family, friends, and community all cherishing him and thanking God for the beauty of his life, which we knew would go on forever. We were blessed by a strong, faithful community that supported us. Our faith was strong and unwavering; however, the days and weeks that followed were not easy. They were filled with sadness, and I felt as though I would never be happy again.

My sister, Kathy, and her husband, Keith, had lost their one-year-old son suddenly three-and-a-half years earlier to a rare and fatal virus. At the time I was a senior in college, newly engaged to be married, and pretty wrapped up in my own life. I was heartbroken that my little nephew and godson had died, but after the funeral, I went back to my own life, while my sister's was forever changed. I had no clue what she was going through. I had no idea what it was like to love your own child - that overwhelming, intense, all-consuming, unconditional love for your child. A love that only a parent understands.

Three years later, broken by my own grief, I finally thought of my sister and what she had gone through. Thinking about how hopeless and desperate I was, I felt so terrible for her, and wondered if she had been in this much pain all this time. I remember calling her and apologizing to her for not being more supportive and compassionate toward her in her grief. She was then, and always has been, a huge support for me. We shared our grief. We talked about how at first it took every ounce of her energy just to breathe and keep living, but that in time, her heart did heal and joy did gradually return. She gave me hope that someday I would feel joy again. She was right.

My grief came hard right away and Chris was able to be really supportive and help me through it. His grief hit him harder later. So it was really a blessing for us because when I was weak, he was strong, and when he was weak, I was strong. God truly blessed us and brought us through the grief, strengthening our marriage and our faith.

NICOLE BERNADETTE ALFARO
January 28, 1993

About seven months after losing Trini, I became pregnant with our third child. I remember thinking that since the only time I had with Trini was the pregnancy, I did not want to waste a moment. I wanted to enjoy and cherish every minute of this pregnancy. I remember telling people, "I'm going to love this baby while I can, because it may be the only time I get with this child." Though I very clearly remember thinking and feeling that, deep down I wasn't worried and never in a million years thought it would be true.

I had an ultrasound during the pregnancy, and we were told that she was a girl. Very excited, we named her Nicole Bernadette. From that day on she was not just "the baby;" she was Nicole. Our oldest son, Michael, was now three, and he hugged and kissed my tummy every night, hugging and kissing his baby sister, Nicole.

At a later point in the pregnancy, during another ultrasound, the technician kept looking at something specific. I asked her what she was looking at. She said she just wanted to have the doctor look at one of the baby's kidneys. The doctor came in, looked at it briefly and said, "it's fine." Nothing was ever mentioned again, and I never thought about it after that.

When it came time for delivery, Nicole was breech. The doctor tried to turn her but was unable. I had an amazing Catholic doctor who actually allowed me to try to deliver her vaginally even though she was breech and my two prior deliveries had been C-sections. Many doctors would never have allowed that. It was such a blessing. We didn't even realize at the time what an amazing gift it would end up being for us.

On January 28, 1993, I went into the OB for my regular visit. I had been having small contractions, but nothing too consistent. Truthfully, I hadn't really been paying much attention because we had just moved into a new apartment the day before and had so much work to do. I only had three-and-a-half weeks left to get everything settled before Nicole was due. When the doctor checked my cervix, I was already dilated to four centimeters. He sent us right to the hospital. I asked him if I could at least go home and pack a suitcase first. The answer was no, because Nicole was breech. Being dilated to four, if my water were to break, her feet could slide right out, so instead of the list of things we had planned get done that day, we went straight to the hospital to have our baby. Because she was breech, the doctor told me I had to have an epidural and deliver her in the operating room in case he had to quickly do a C-section. Apparently, once any part of the baby is born, there is a limited amount of time to get the rest of the baby out safely. So if Nicole's body was born and then her shoulders or head got stuck, the doctor would need to quickly do a C-section. Originally, we had wanted to do all natural births without medication, but now, for Nicole's safety, I had to have an epidural. In truth, I loved it. My husband loved it. I could have played cards during labor. The medicine allowed me to enjoy labor and delivery, which was exciting and peaceful after having had such a difficult and traumatic labor with Michael.

My husband, Chris, is half Mexican and has beautiful dark skin, hair, and eyes, and I always thought his little sisters were adorable. I remember telling the nurse that I would love to have a daughter that looked like them, with that gorgeous tan skin and dark hair and eyes. I told her that would be my "dream girl."

As I anticipated her arrival into the world, I was overjoyed that this was going to be my first vaginal birth, with all the beauty that entailed. Even though Nicole was breech, her delivery was surprisingly smooth. Rather than having to wait a long time for the head to crown, she just seemed to slide out easily. She was a double footling breech, meaning both feet were down and came out first. The moment she was born was amazing beyond words. It truly was a miracle. After the two previous C-sections and trauma, Nicole's birth brought the most intense joy I had ever felt. As soon as the nurse saw her, she said, "You got your dream girl!" What joy filled that room. What joy filled our hearts. I remember just crying out, "Thank you, Jesus! Thank you, Jesus!" over and over.

The joy quickly turned, though, as Nicole didn't cry. She struggled to breathe and only the tiniest little squeaks came out when she tried to cry. They placed her in my husband's arms and allowed him to carry her to the nursery where they were going to give her some oxygen support. The doctor told me that it was quite normal for babies born breech to have trouble breathing at first. Apparently, there is something about the way the lungs are compressed when they come out head first that helps get the lungs started. So, without that, breech babies often need a little help breathing at first.

Chris came back to me while doctors worked to get Nicole settled. We were told that she had pneumothorax, which is a rupture in the lung. They would have to put a chest tube in to drain the air from her chest so that her lung would be able to expand as she breathed. We were told that this was all pretty common after a breech delivery. We called Chris's mom who is a nurse, and she didn't seem alarmed by any of it. She agreed it was fairly usual.

We waited and waited. As the wait got longer and longer, we inquired with the nurses, asking if there was a need for us to baptize her right away. The nurses were all very calm. One took a picture of Nicole with a polaroid camera and brought it to us for comfort. Finally, the nurses were ready to move me out of the delivery room into a regular room. As we were leaving, she said, "We will stop by the nursery on our way to your room. That way you can see your baby and put your mind at ease."

We found Nicole, however, not in the nursery; she was the Neonatal Intensive Care Unit (NICU). We walked in and were met by a doctor saying, "I'm sure you know by now that your baby is in critical condition. She has one of three things, and if it's what we think, she will steadily go downhill until she dies." No, we did not know. We were completely stunned. They brought us over to our precious little Nicole, who by this point had been medically paralyzed, had her eyes covered, was hooked up to a respirator, IV, and several other monitors. This little baby girl who had just been moving and kicking inside me was now lying there fighting for her life. Needless to say, we never made it to my room.

Chris baptized her immediately. Father John, our parish priest and close friend, came as quickly as he could and finished all of the baptismal prayers. Family began to travel to Milwaukee from Michigan, and prayers were being said all over the country for our little Nicole. We never left her side that night.

The next morning, the doctors decided to transport her to the local children's hospital, where she could receive the best care possible. Because my doctor had allowed me to deliver Nicole vaginally, I was able to stand at her bedside all night and then be discharged the next morning so that I could stay with her. If I had had a C-section, I would not have been able to spend all that time, what would turn out to be my only time, with Nicole.

For thirty hours we rode a rollercoaster of emotions as we prayed with, sang to, caressed, and loved our newborn daughter. Our hearts were overflowing with love for our little girl. We stood by her bedside and talked to her and prayed for her. Her vital signs went up when we were with her. She knew us. She needed us. There were moments of great grace and strength, and then moments of weakness when we would wrestle with our own human fatigue, fear, and doubt. We wondered how long we could keep this up, torn between our dying infant in the hospital and our three-year-old son at home. Then the guilt would come. So many conflicting and overwhelming emotions consumed us.

Early in the morning on January 30, two days after she had been born, the doctors told us nothing was working. They asked if we wanted them to take her off the machines so we could hold her before she died. This was all so new to us. We didn't know what our moral responsibility was in this situation. So we asked them to continue to do everything possible until we could talk to my dad about it. Before we could make any decisions, though, Nicole couldn't fight any longer and went home to Jesus and her brother, Trini. How I longed to hold her, but when I finally got her in my arms, it was so evident she was gone. I felt a huge difference between when she was lying there alive and after she had died. Her little baby body was in my arms, but she was gone. It was a stark reality. In thirty hours, I went from the greatest, highest peak of joy to the lowest, deepest sorrow I could imagine. It felt like complete devastation, total tragedy. Just like that, my dream girl was gone.

In some ways, I was embarrassed and felt deceived by God. There I had been, just thirty hours earlier, thanking Him, and all along He knew He was going to snatch her away from me and crush me. I was devastated. I had always had a bit of a hard time showing emotion in front of people, and after this, I withdrew even more, hesitant to show any emotion, particularly excitement or joy.

Despite the hurt, however, neither of us became really angry with God. We had amazing support from our family and parish community. Our faith was strong, and we trusted God's love for us and His plan for our lives. We were thankful that we had at least a little time with Nicole while she was alive. I remember Chris standing up and sharing at Nicole's funeral. He talked about when he was able to walk Nicole to the nursery. He said that she was fussing, struggling to breathe and trying to cry. He looked at her and said, "Shh, it's okay." Nicole looked up at him and settled right down. It was obvious that she recognized his voice and was comforted by him. Chris stood in front of our family and friends and community and said, "For that one moment, I would do it all over again." I am so thankful to have a husband who is such a loving father and so committed to God and the sanctity and beauty of all life.

Nicole's autopsy confirmed that she had Autosomal Recessive Polycystic Kidney Disease (ARPKD). With ARPKD the kidneys become cystic and enlarged and do not function properly. With the kidneys not functioning properly, the baby does not urinate, and it is the baby's urine that makes up the amniotic fluid in the womb. Consequently, it is the baby breathing in and out the amniotic fluid which helps the lungs develop. So Nicole's lungs ended up being brittle and underdeveloped due to lack of amniotic fluid. That is why she could not breathe on her own after birth. We were also told that ARPKD was a rare but genetic disease, and that each of our subsequent children would have a twenty-five percent chance of developing it in the womb between twenty-three and twenty-eight weeks. So, unlike Trini's rare, not-likely-to-happen-again condition, Nicole's was one we would never be free of. My idea that I needed to enjoy every moment and love them in the womb because that might be all the time I would have was no longer just an ideal; it was a reality that I was going to have to hold onto and live by. I became afraid that I would never have another healthy baby.

The weeks that followed were more than difficult. There is nothing in life that is so permanent as death. It hits like a ton of bricks, because there is absolutely nothing you can do to change the situation. It is final. This time grief hit both Chris and me hard at the same time. It was very difficult because we were used to being able to rely on each other for strength, but when one of us would try to lean on the other, we would fall down. We were both so empty and hurting so much that we had nothing left to give. One week, grief peaked for both of us at the same time. It was scary. I was so caught up in my own pain that I couldn't see his. All I could see was that he wasn't there for me when I needed him most. I wondered how we would ever make it through.

I had heard that many marriages fall apart after the loss of a child. I never understood it. It seemed to me that losing a child was bad enough; why would you want to let go of your best friend and spouse, too? Well, for that one week, I finally understood how this might happen. Each grieving parent gets so wrapped up in his or her own pain, and is entirely unable to support the other. Both end up hurt because it appears the other person isn't caring for you when you need them so desperately. It is only by clinging to God and letting Him lift you up that you can get through it.

Not only were Chris and I grieving, but Michael was too. Michael was a deeply spiritual little boy. He was also very good at expressing himself, even at only three years old. I remember sitting on my bed with him, and he said, "I'm mad!" I asked him who he was mad at. I was surprised when he responded, "I'm mad at Nicole for leaving me!" It was so hard to see his pain. He had waited for two siblings and lost them both. Miraculously, however, the Lord blessed him with an amazing gift: every time we went into a church, Michael saw, near the crucifix, Jesus holding two babies, Trini and Nicole. Oh, how I wished I could have seen what he saw, but I never did. It went on for months. It simply became common and ordinary for him to see them there. What an amazing gift. He had a child's faith and such a pure heart. He began then to pray every day for another baby brother or sister. After a few months, I noticed he had stopped. When I asked him why, he said he didn't need to anymore because we already had one. He was right. On Mother's Day, 1993, we found out I was pregnant again.

ANDREA ELIZABETH ALFARO
January 5, 1994

Despite the fact that I had just lost two babies in a row, my next pregnancy was pretty peaceful. I have been blessed with very easy pregnancies compared to many women. It was an emotional rollercoaster of hope and fear, but overall, I had peace. I had an ultrasound at twenty weeks and we found out we had another daughter. We were so happy! We named her Andrea Elizabeth. She looked great on the ultrasound, but ARPKD doesn't typically begin to develop until about twenty-three weeks. We were told that if the disease hadn't developed by twenty-eight weeks, it wouldn't. So, the plan was to have another ultrasound at twenty-eight weeks to check her kidneys. We were thankful for every day we had with Andrea, but as the day of her ultrasound drew closer, there was much fear, not knowing whether we would get to keep her or be forced to let her go and give her back to the Lord.

On October 27th, the day before my twenty-sixth birthday and the day of our new niece's birth, we went in to have Andrea's twenty-eight-week ultrasound. I was so nervous. I didn't know what I would do or how I would handle it if we found out Andrea had the kidney disease. Waiting was awful. When we got into the ultrasound, the technician studied every little organ and measured her amniotic fluid and told us everything was perfect! Little Andrea looked perfectly healthy. Our relief and excitement were beyond words. We could actually really let ourselves get excited to have another baby. According to the doctors, there shouldn't be any reason to not have a healthy baby this time.

Along with the twenty-eight-week ultrasound, I also required non-stress tests in the last two months of my pregnancy. Doctors monitored the baby and her environment very closely toward the end since they had no idea why Trini had died in the womb. All of my non-stress tests with Andrea were very good, but as my due date drew closer, my nerves became more and more tense. After losing two babies in a row and not knowing why Trini had died, we just wanted to get baby Andrea out alive and healthy while we could. Two weeks before my due date my doctor induced labor. Physically it wasn't really necessary, but for peace of mind it was a gift.

We had decided that I would have an epidural again. It wasn't quite as magical this time around. It only worked halfway, blocking the pain on only one side of my body. Eventually they figured it out, and put in a new epidural which worked great. I ended up having a good labor and delivery with her, and the sound of her cry filled the room and our hearts with unexplainable joy and gratitude. She had beautiful dark skin and hair just like her sister, Nicole. What an amazing miracle and gift. Our prayers had been answered. We were truly blessed! Andrea Elizabeth was born on January 5th, the day between the feast of St. Andre and Saint Elizabeth Ann Seton. How perfect.

With Andrea being born less than a year after Nicole, I was very aware that if Nicole had lived, Andrea would most likely not have been conceived. When I breastfeed, I do not get my periods back, so it basically would have been impossible. I began to see some of the beauty in God's plan in the fact that now they would both have life for all eternity. I became so grateful for both of my precious daughters and the life they had been given.

Michael, too, adored his little sister. He snuggled her and loved her and played with her. After four years of being the only child, some jealousy would be normal, but there was none. There was just total admiration. I think he appreciated her more than most siblings ever think to. He was a very loving and protective big brother. As Andrea grew, she adored Michael as well. She looked out for him too in her own little way. From very early on, we noticed how giving Andrea was. Everything she ever had or was given, she was sure to share with Michael, whether he asked for it or not.

Having both Michael and Andrea was a complete joy. With Michael four years old, the adjustment to two children was really very easy. Michael and Andrea were quiet and well-behaved children. They looked out for each other, shared naturally, and really cared for each other. Life was good, and Chris and I (being still young and naive) thought we were pretty good parents. Obviously, humility was still something we needed to learn.

SETH THOMAS ALFARO

August 23, 1995

Just one year later, I was pregnant again. This time I was actually afraid to be pregnant. I felt like it was too soon. Life was easy now. I wondered if I could even handle two babies so close together. It also felt like we might not be able to handle another loss at the time. Such conflicting emotions: we were afraid to have another baby and afraid to lose one all at the same time. Human emotion is often so contradictory and selfish. Thank goodness my mom always taught me that emotions are not necessarily right or wrong. They're just there, and it is what we do with them that counts. No matter what I feel, God knows what I can and can't handle better than I do. So we prayed for the health and safety of our unborn baby as well as the grace to handle whatever God asked of us. We tried to trust as we rode that emotional roller coaster up and down once again for six months until the dreaded twenty-eight-week ultrasound. We had never had two healthy babies in a row. Was it even possible?

At twenty-eight weeks, I braved the ultrasound on my own since Chris was busy at work. It was a scary time. We were not emotionally or spiritually prepared for bad news. From my point of view, things had to be good because at that time in our lives I really feared that another loss may break us. My sister offered to go with me, but I really just wanted to be alone. I received the blessed news that our little baby boy was healthy. We named him Seth Thomas. In the Bible, Seth is the third son of Adam and Eve, after they lost their second son. We thought it was a fitting name for our third son, after having lost our second.

Toward the end of the pregnancy, I had non-stress tests twice a week just like I did with Nicole and Andrea. While most of them were good, there was one that was not. The doctors determined Seth was okay, but every possible little problem was enough to set my already raw nerves on edge.

As the time for delivery approached, Seth was in the breech position. The doctor tried to turn him but was unable, just like with Nicole. This made me nervous as well. It was all too reminiscent of a scenario we did not want to revisit. Tension was high the morning of August 23, 1995 as we drove to the hospital to deliver our son, Seth Thomas. I had another epidural, but this time the epidural got into my system and made me very sick. I was vomiting all through labor and delivery. It was awful. I felt so sick that I could barely even focus on the fact that I was having a baby. Seth was franklin breech, which meant that he came out butt first with both legs completely tucked up next to his body. Gratefully, as the doctors had said, Seth was healthy. Although I was sick, he had a perfect breech delivery, and no pneumothorax or trouble breathing at all. His cry was loud and strong and so beautiful.

Seth came out full of energy, and has continued to have it every day of his life. Our quiet little family wasn't so quiet anymore. We have always joked that we should have known what we were in for when he came out butt first. Seth filled our home with life and vigor. He did everything all the way. There was no middle ground. When he was happy, he was really happy and filled our home with joy; however, when he was mad, he was really mad, and it didn't matter where we were. We began to learn a little bit about humility as parents through our tough, yet sensitive, little Sethy Thomas.

JOHN DAVID ALFARO
December 26, 1997

In the Spring of 1997, I became pregnant again. Michael was seven. Andrea was three, and Seth was one-and-a-half. As with every pregnancy since Nicole's, we began that emotional rollercoaster of excitement and anticipation, as well as fear and worry. At around twenty weeks, we found out the baby was a boy. We named him John David. We called him baby Jack. It became very special for us to name our babies as soon as we knew whether we were having a girl or boy. It helped us bond with them and know them and feel closer to them for as long as we could. We learned to value and treasure every moment we had with each one.

Everything seemed to be going along well, and the twenty-eighth week was quickly approaching. The weekend before my ultrasound, I went on a silent women's retreat. With three young children at home, the silence was an amazing gift. There was beautiful prayer time and inspirational talks. Even the meals were in silence. On Saturday night, the priest was offering the Sacrament of the Sick during the evening prayer service. Earlier in the day, Father had told me that I could receive the sacrament for healing of the genetic kidney condition that could be passed on to our babies, and for healing of the baby I was carrying in case he actually had the disease. That night, during the prayer service, I went to the front of the church with several of the other women and was anointed. No one knew anyone else's struggles or reasons for being anointed.

Sunday after Mass, the silence was allowed to be broken as we all packed up and got ready to leave. A woman I did not know knocked on my door. She introduced herself and proceeded to tell me the reason for her visit. She said, "I don't know what your situation is, but last night when you were anointed, I felt like God wanted me to tell you that it won't be easy, but that He will be with you through it all." I know she meant well, but I did not want to hear what she had to say. I honestly was so angry. Truthfully, I wanted to punch her in the face. She didn't know me. She had no idea what I had been through and what her words meant for me. My ultrasound was scheduled for Thursday. Any peace I had gained during the retreat was instantly gone . . .

For the next four days, I was in agony, filled with fear at the thought of what her words could mean. With great apprehension we went to the doctor Thursday morning for my ultrasound. The technician turned on the ultrasound but immediately turned it off and said, "I'm going to go get the doctor." The doctor came in, took one look at the baby with the ultrasound and gave us the news that we had feared and dreaded and prayed we would never have to hear. Our baby had Autosomal Recessive Polycystic Kidney Disease (ARPKD), like Nicole. We were told that John David would die shortly after birth. There was nothing they could do for him. There was no hope other than an outright miracle.

With Trini and Nicole, we had no warning. I always wondered how I would handle it, if I ever got this news ahead of time. How would I prepare for the birth and death of my child? I was afraid I may not be able to bond with him for fear of the pain of losing him. The beginning was filled with tears and sadness, which quickly turned into prayers of desperation. I began to beg and plead with the Lord to heal my baby.

All through the Gospels, Jesus healed person after person. He often said that their faith healed them. So I started to think that if I believed enough, John David would be healed. My mom had experienced physical miracles like that, and in fact I had too when I was in second grade. After months of strep throat that nothing would cure, I was sent in to have my tonsils removed. The night before my surgery, some friends from church prayed over me, asking for healing. The next day, the doctor looked at my tonsils and said they were perfectly healthy and didn't need to come out. I still have them to this day. Then, when I was a senior in high school, after many years of illness, my mom was sent home from the hospital to die. Doctors weren't able to do anything else for her. Five days before my sister's wedding, however, my mom was miraculously healed. Miracles of healing weren't foreign to me. So I began to read the Gospels, paying special attention to the miracles. I also listened to recordings that my parents had of speakers talking about miraculous healings.

For the next two months, I prayed and begged and pleaded with all my heart and soul. Here is an excerpt from my prayer journal after I had read Matthew 15:30–31, which reads:

> Great crowds came to him having with them the lame, the blind, the deformed, the mute, and many others. They placed them at His feet, and He cured them. The crowds were amazed when they saw the mute speaking, the deformed made whole, the lame walking, and the blind able to see, and they glorified the God of Israel.

December 14, 1997

Dear Lord,

Please let this passage come to be for us and John David. We bring him to You and place him at Your feet, Please, we beg You, heal him. I believe that so many many people will be amazed, and we will give all the honor and glory to You. And I believe many doctors, nurses, and even strangers could be changed and converted and begin to glorify You.

I know You desire to heal and that sickness is not Your will. It entered the world with sin. But I also know that You can bring good out of any situation. Through Nicole's death, Andrea was able to have life. Now, they both may have eternal life. Sometimes I feel like in order for John David to be healed, I have to believe without a doubt that it is Your will to heal him. But who am I to know Your will? If this is a lack of faith please help me. I believe with all my heart that You can heal John David in a split second. You are the author of life. Only You know what is ultimately best and what will bring You the most honor and glory and turn more people toward You to be saved. So, I feel like I can't be certain of what Your will is for John David and us in this situation. If I am wrong please show me and direct me. I just place myself and my family at Your mercy and just beg You and plead with You to heal this precious baby boy, John David, whom You have lent to us. Please, please, please let him be born alive and healthy and come home with us and share our lives and home. And let many people be amazed and give glory to You and allow no more abortions to be done at the hospital here and even in the whole city. Let word of Your divine healing power spread throughout the country and use us as witnesses. And also, please let this miracle aid in the process of the canonization of Mother Teresa of Calcutta. Have pity on us, O Lord Jesus, and heal this special baby and let his life bear witness to You just as St. John the Baptist did. Please Lord, I beg You to heal him and let him live with us, and all of us proclaim the glory of God. I ask and pray all this in Jesus' name. Amen.

This is how I prayed constantly, begging for healing and asking for the faith to truly believe God would heal my baby. We also grew in prayer as a family. We knelt down every night together and prayed a family rosary. Also, there were literally people all over the country praying for us. We had even contacted the Sisters of Charity and they were all praying for us. We were particularly invoking Mother Teresa's intercession. We hoped this miracle could be attributed to her intercession and help aid in her canonization. It was a very grace-filled two months for our family. I had been afraid that the two months of waiting for his birth might be terribly painful and that I wouldn't be able to bond with the baby. I thought maybe every time I felt him move it would make me sad, but the opposite happened. Every movement I felt filled me with incredible joy and gratitude for John David's life.

After two months of pleading and seeking, I really did believe that God was going to heal John David. I even told people so. I was ready to proclaim God's greatness to the world. I had grandiose plans. This miracle was going to change hearts, and John David's life was going to be a witness to all people and many would be converted and proclaim God's power and majesty. It was a perfect plan, right?

During this time, we also met with the neonatologists to discuss what they might be able to do for John David after his birth. We knew the prognosis was death, but we wanted doctors to have the opportunity to examine him and know for sure what was really going on. We didn't want to just assume and let him go without giving him every fighting chance to survive. The doctors agreed to intubate John David and put him on a respirator to help him breathe right away while they assessed his situation.

At one point I started to have some signs of labor, and it was definitely too early. I called the doctor's office, and told them what was happening and asked them what I should do. The response was shocking to me. The doctor wasn't worried because, after all, the baby was going to die anyway. We felt entirely differently: John David was our child to love and protect while we could. If he died from ARPKD, there would be nothing we could do, but we certainly weren't going to let him die for some other reason without doing everything in our power to save him. We felt like they were treating his life as if it didn't matter, like they had already written him off. So, I put myself on bedrest until things settled down, just like the doctor would have done if John David had been healthy.

On Christmas day, I started to have contractions. Normally this would have been very exciting, but in this case there was great fear and trepidation. I remember praying, "Lord, if I am not going to get my miracle, please don't let him be born on Christmas day." Sadly, shortly after my prayer, my contractions stopped. I did not want to even think about what that could mean.

The day after Christmas I went into full labor. Physically this was one of my most difficult labors because the epidural didn't work at all, so I felt everything. Emotionally it was unbelievably difficult as well. While I was in labor at the hospital, the neonatologist who was on duty came into my room and proceeded to tell Chris and me that we were being selfish. He couldn't believe we wanted John David to be intubated and put on a respirator to help him breathe. He essentially told us it was cruel to put the baby through that. How could we make him suffer so? He thought we should just accept that he was dying and hold him and let him go. Those words were so hard to hear, and I really couldn't handle them while I was in labor to deliver our dying son. Why did all the neonatologists agree to intubate him when we met with them earlier? That is why we had met with them ahead of time. I'm not sure why it happened the way it did, but God worked it out. That doctor went off duty right before John David was born, and the doctor who came on duty was so kind and compassionate toward us and cared for John David with great dignity and love.

John David, like Nicole and Seth, was also breech. He was single footling, meaning one foot came out first and the other one was tucked straight up against his body. When he was born, he did not cry. He was struggling to breathe. The doctor immediately took him and intubated him right there and began helping him breathe.

Our pastor, Father Jim, waited outside the delivery room, and as soon as he was allowed, he came in the room and baptized John David for us. Then they brought the baby over to me, and I gave him a quick hug and a kiss goodbye, and just like that he was taken away to the neonatal intensive care unit. I just remember how good he felt. His little body was so warm and cuddly. I held onto that moment in my heart.

The next time we saw our baby, he was hooked up to machines just like Nicole had been. As nurses explained his situation, Chris and I touched him and caressed him, our hearts breaking once again. My Dad and my brother and sister-in-law were also there with Michael and Andrea. We placed the Miraculous Medal on John David's chest, and my Dad reached over and began to pray over him. As John David settled in, the nurses told us that if there was any hope it would be a long haul and this was probably going to be the best he would be for a while. Since by this time it was late at night, we decided that we had better try to get some sleep while he was stable. Chris went home to be with our other children, and I went to my room to try to sleep a little. I was awakened very early by a phone call from the doctors saying that John David had taken a turn for the worse. I called Chris and he came immediately. We were told that, despite all that the doctors were doing, John David's oxygen would not stay at a level that would sustain life. He was dying.

By this time, it was around six o'clock on Saturday morning. Several of our family members came, and they brought Michael and Andrea too. I remember my mom was sick with the flu, and it was heartbreaking for her not to have been there the night before. That morning I told her to come. It was the end and she did not need to worry about exposing little John David to her illness. This would be her only chance to be with him.

Our hope in medical science was gone. The doctors and nurses took John David off all the machines, so we could hold him and love him until he died. Father Jim came and prayed all the prayers for the dying, and prayed over Chris and me as we held him and cried. As Father Jim prayed, I continued to beg God for a miracle. He could heal him without the help of medical science. There was absolutely no acceptance in my heart of the fact that my baby was dying. In fact, in all my prayers, begging and pleading, never once did I pray as Jesus did, "Your will, not mine, be done."

John David's heartbeat slowed way down until it finally beat for the very last time while his eight-year-old big brother, Michael, held him in his arms. Andrea (almost four) sat next to Michael in the hospital rocking chair with John David's little feet and blanket draped across her lap. As the nurse pronounced him dead, my husband, Chris, who was kneeling on the floor in front of the rocker with John David's little hand in his, hung his head in sorrow. It was over. Only thirteen hours after his birth, our baby boy was gone, and no amount of praying was going to bring him back.

The following is a poem written by my sister for Michael. She says it was inspired by John David, after she watched him die in Michael's arms:

"To My Big Brother...Until We Meet Again"

Today when you first held me
And I saw your tender smile
I felt like I had known you
For a very, very long while.

I knew your gentle voice
From the times you've talked to me
You sounded so very special
I just couldn't wait to see.

I knew your touch
Before today too
From the loving little kindnesses
You used to do.

The blessings and kisses
And gentle little hugs
You gave me as you nestled
Into Mommy so snug.
I'd guessed you were special
And today I knew it was true
What a wonderful brother
God gave me in you.

You held me in your sweet embrace
Your arms around me tight
Hugging and loving and praying
For me with all your might.

And your prayers were answered

Although it may not have seemed so
For God had another place
He wished for me to go.

And although I didn't want
To leave you just quite now
I knew that God had other plans
In store for me somehow.

But one thing I am sure of
You can count it as a fact
You'll hold me in your arms again
When I can hold you back.

We'll talk and laugh together then
And be the best of friends
God has all the answers, Brother,
The "hows," the "whys," the "whens."

So let Him take away the pain
Take comfort in His grace
Know we'll meet again in Heaven
You, God, and me, face to face.
Keep loving as only you can do
Be kind to Andrea and Seth, "Bro"
And give Mommy and Daddy a great big hug
From me, when they're feeling low.

And remember...
There's one thing I am sure of
You can count it as a fact
You will hold me in your arms again
But next time, I'll be holding you back.

Our whole family stayed there in the NICU room for quite
a long while. The hospital staff left us alone, and we all took time

to hug and love and caress little John David. I didn't even realize it at the time, but my sister, Kathy, took lots of pictures during it all. What an incredible gift to have now. After everyone had a chance to hold and snuggle John David and say goodbye, they left. I was alone rocking my newborn son for the very last time. This time, I didn't feel like he was gone, like I had felt so strongly with Nicole. I felt like he was still there with me, and I did not want to let him go. I do not know how much time passed, but it must have been quite a while. The nurses were very kind and patient, but they finally had to make me give him up. It was agonizing to let him go knowing that I would never hold my baby again.

As with any death, despite the devastation, the next few days were extremely busy with funeral arrangements. Here we were again, planning a funeral for another one of our children. I'm sure the funeral must have been beautiful like the others, but there was something very different this time. I felt no peace, no comfort at all from God. Usually, that was the only thing that got me through. What was happening to me? I knew the truth, that God's plan is always best and the most loving, but it sure didn't feel like it. I was hurt. I was numb.

I had never really questioned God before, but this time my heart was filled with questions. What was God doing to me? After all, I had always trusted God. I believed in God's awesome power. All through the Gospels, Jesus healed people. And He said, "ask and you shall receive." Well, I asked, I begged, I pleaded with the Lord for two months to heal my baby. And I believed that He would. But He didn't. That's all I could see, and it crushed me. I proposed, and God disposed according to *His* will, not mine. And I was having a very difficult time accepting that.

Grief was really different this time. I didn't know how to feel. I couldn't feel. It was too painful. Part of me felt like maybe it should be easy because after all, I had already been through it twice before. I should be a pro. The other part of me knew how painful it was and just didn't want to face it again. I was afraid to grieve, afraid of the intense pain. As time went on, I simply grew more and more numb. Even my eight-year-old, Michael, commented that I looked the same when I was happy as when I was sad.

Chris and the kids were also grieving. Michael was in second grade at the time, and his teacher told me that he often looked sad and would just sit alone on the bench during recess. He also became very afraid of things, especially at night. We began family counseling for him with a friend from our church who is a child psychologist. It was extremely helpful for him and all of us. It forced us to talk about our feelings and work through them together. It was sometimes very hard for Chris to talk about it. In fact, if I was having a bad day, he would call my mom and ask her if she could take me to lunch or something because he knew I really needed to talk. Our friend once asked Chris what the worst and best parts of counseling were for him. The answer was the same for both. He said he hated having to open up and share his feelings, yet it was so good when he did. Having to share such deep emotions was so difficult, yet so beneficial. For disliking it so much, he was actually very good at it. I think it was so difficult for him because he actually put his whole self into it and didn't just keep it superficial.

Andrea also, at age four, was trying to process it in her own way. These are her bedtime prayer intentions from one night just a week and a half after John David (baby Jack) died: "That we can have a baby girl, and she won't die; that I (Andrea) can die and go live in Heaven with Trini, Nicole, and Jack; that Jesus can do magic and heal Jack and make him all better so he can come back and live with us."

As much as I wanted to be, I don't think I was much help to the kids. As time passed, I literally felt like I was dying inside, no matter how much I talked or prayed about it. I hated who I was becoming. I felt completely empty and dead inside. I had a husband and three children to care for, but I felt like I had nothing to give them. I could do and say all the right things, like hold them and tell them I loved them, but I felt nothing. I didn't know what to do. I didn't know what was happening to me, and I didn't really know how to express any of it. I was really afraid I would never come through it. A friend of mine suggested that I write a letter to God, as my friend, and just tell Him all I was feeling and experiencing.

I typically journal a lot during my prayer. So I decided to take my friend's advice and began to write a letter to God in my journal. Usually as I journal, I write pretty neatly and am fairly guarded and careful about what I write. This time, however, all the anger, confusion, and pain inside me just flowed out unguarded. My writing became very sloppy as the pen just flowed without restraint. I finally realized and admitted for the first time that I was really angry with God. The letter from the beginning of this book was what came out that day, re-printed here:

March 30, 1998

Dear Lord,

I buried John David three months ago - and with him I feel I've buried a huge part of myself. I feel dead inside. I feel so broken and only sadness in the numbness. I feel so trapped inside - so alone - it's like I've buried all that I feel and like I'll never feel [alive] again. I already had a problem with showing joy and making myself vulnerable in that way. Now it's just getting worse and worse. You keep crushing my joy. I feel like You're stomping the life right out of me. I know in my head that You are not trying to hurt me - but it does hurt! I know there must be something You can teach me in all this - but I hate it. I'm so afraid that I won't come through this - that I'll be lost forever. I hate who I am right now, but I feel powerless to change it. I know that You can change it, not me, but it is hard to seek You. I feel like You've allowed all this and then abandoned me. Maybe it's me who abandoned You - but it's hard to come to You for comfort - knowing that You didn't have to let this happen. You could have changed it all - I wanted You to - I begged You to, and I believed - I trusted that You would heal my baby - but You didn't. Why not? ... Why did You lead me to believe in the miracle, knowing that You weren't going to do it? You smashed my hope and my joy once again. How much must I bear? How long will You continue to tear apart my heart and stomp on my joy? I know You are trying to help me and teach me, but that doesn't make me feel any better. In fact, it makes me feel worse, because then I feel like it's wrong to be mad and hurt. I hate that I can't understand. I hate that I have to try to live divinely, when I am only human and can't possibly even begin to understand.

I want to be a woman of joy - but I'm not. I've become a cold, numb, dead person inside. I hate the kind of wife and mother I've become. I want to feel. I want to be true to myself and others. I want to be alive. I want joy. I'm so sick of feeling this way - of not feeling and not expressing. I want to laugh even if no one else does. I want a smile to be my normal. I want to cry and cry and cry and release all the death within me.

I know I need You - but the thought of making up with You is so hard to bear - because I feel so hurt by You - so mad. Where are You? I don't feel You anymore. I just feel sadness and <u>so so so</u> alone. You hurt me. You led me with false joy and hope for two months, knowing full well how crushed I was going to be. I know You didn't try to crush me - that it's all for good - but that doesn't take away the pain and how I feel. I hurt. I'm <u>so</u> hurt by You. **Where are You?** I'm left alone now - I don't want to die inside, but I feel like I am. I'm afraid to be this way. I'm afraid it won't ever change. I'm afraid of who I've become - I hate it!

Sometimes when I hold the kids, I feel cold and withdrawn and like I'm an empty vessel holding them - like I'm not even there. I feel so alone, so withdrawn. I feel like I'm lost, and I'm afraid that I will be lost forever. I don't want to be this way. But even when I feel like I'm doing this to the kids, I still can't find my heart and give it to them. This scares me. It's got to affect them. I don't want to hurt them. I want to feel them and them to feel me.

Even though I am angry and hurt, please come to me. I know I need You. Don't leave me alone. Don't abandon me, and don't let me abandon You. I need You. I want to feel Your presence. I need to feel Your presence. I don't want to be alone, and I don't want the children to be alone without me. Please help me. Mend my broken heart. Help me to feel and experience the joys and pains of this life and be true to them and live and feel through them ... Pull me back to You. Please embrace me, and let me feel Your love. Show Your love to me and bring me back to life again - even more vibrant and alive than before. Heal all the hurts. Make me true to who I am...

Writing the letter was so good for me. I finally expressed all that had been trapped inside me for the past three months since John David had died. I was finally honest with myself and God. Up to that point I didn't even realize how angry I was, because I couldn't admit it. I was a good Catholic. How could I question God? Well, good Catholic or not, this was how I felt. Yes, I knew God was perfect, knew what was best for me, and was all-loving, but I couldn't change the way I felt. I was hurt and could not understand what He was doing to me and why.

I wrote the letter, but I couldn't close it. I couldn't sign it. So I just waited and held on to it, along with all the anger and hurt. I knew I needed God, but could not let go of those intense feelings of hurt, anger, and resentment. I felt like God had punched me in the gut, so how could I go running to Him for comfort? While I kept praying and asking for God's help, I knew I was not willing to let go and trust in His love and His will.

After a few days of carrying around what I now knew was this intense anger toward God, I just couldn't do it anymore. Having actually admitted and identified the anger and realizing that I couldn't do this on my own, I was finally ready to let it go. On the evening of April 1, I went to the Eucharistic Adoration Chapel at our church. I knelt down, and I said, "Lord, I give this anger to You. I can't do this on my own. I need You, and I want

You." The letting go wasn't based on a feeling, but a decision. The feelings followed. I could finally honestly say that I wanted the Lord and wanted and needed to be in close relationship with Him. For the first time since I found out John David had ARPKD and was going to die, I let go of my will and accepted God's. It was so freeing. As soon as I let go, God's love came rushing into my heart again. I remember feeling like a young girl newly in love. A joy returned to my heart that I had been missing for a very long time. This didn't automatically take away the pain I had from losing John David, but it gave me the grace and strength to begin to walk through the grief.

Later that week, I went to confession to confess my anger and fully make amends with God. Father Jim looked at me and said, "Oh Chris, you have not offended God. He understands your pain; however, when we hold on to anger in our hearts, His love can't get through. We can't receive it." He went on then to describe exactly what had been happening to me over the past three months, without me even telling him about it. God wanted to heal me and fill me with joy, but I would not let Him as long as I was holding such anger and resentment toward Him. Father told me that while we propose many things for our lives, God alone disposes. When we accept and surrender to how God disposes, then He can and will delight us in His will. For my penance, he told me to go home and individually hold each of my children and pray, "Lord, I will propose many things for this child throughout his/her life, but You alone dispose and delight me in it." It was a difficult, but beautiful and very meaningful thing to have to do, verbally and consciously surrendering each of my children to God. It would still be a few years, however, before I would really grasp how God could and would delight me in His will, if I would just surrender.

ETHAN PEDRO ALFARO
December 31, 1998

One year after losing John David, we were blessed with another son, Ethan Pedro. The pregnancy, as always, was twenty-eight weeks of joy and fear, waiting to find out if this new baby would be healthy and be able to stay with us. After losing John David less than a year before, we were more than relieved and overjoyed to find out that our baby boy was healthy! We were so excited and could now actually let ourselves think about and enjoy the reality of having another baby.

On New Year's Eve, 1998, I went into labor. At first things seemed to be going along very smoothly, but then things turned. With every contraction, Ethan's heart would stop beating. Because we kept losing his heart tones, they moved me into the operating room. With me already having an epidural, the doctor would be able to do a C-section in an instant if needed. I was so scared. I was an emotional wreck. I was shaking uncontrollably throughout the rest of the labor and delivery. We knew Ethan was healthy. We just needed to get him out safely. I couldn't lose him too. Just a few hours before midnight, our little Ethan was born, safely and healthy. I was able to deliver him vaginally, but when he came out the cord was wrapped around his neck, which was why his heart stopped with every contraction.

Ethan's birth brought me great joy and healing; my heart was once again filled with joy. I thought I finally understood what Father Jim had said to me about how God would delight me in His will. Yes, God certainly delighted me with Ethan, and I saw that God's plan was perfect because if John David had lived, I most likely would never have had this child. But now, *both* John David and Ethan would have life for all eternity.

Holding my living, breathing, beautiful baby boy was amazing, and tears of joy and thanksgiving flowed. Even being up with him in the middle of the night brought joy. I couldn't complain. Ethan truly blessed our lives. He brought a pure happiness to our home and family. He has always had the most laid-back, happy-go-lucky, friendly personality, as well as the biggest, most adorable smile that melted my heart. God had blessed me so much, and I thought I finally saw and understood how God's plan was perfect. Little did I know how narrow my vision was, and how much more God still had to teach me...

JACOB FRANCIS ALFARO

December 18, 2000

The following year, one Sunday during Lent, I remember Chris and I having a conversation with my mom about having another baby. We were both content, happy, and at peace right where we were. The thought of opening ourselves to loving and losing another child was very scary. Why risk it? Also, many people were actually critical of us every time I became pregnant again. They couldn't understand why we would keep having more children, and they thought we were selfish for continually putting our living children through such heartache.

My mom, being the faithful, holy woman, she was, challenged us to trust God and be open to whatever God willed for our lives. She wasn't saying that God wanted us to have another baby right then, but just didn't want to see us live our lives in fear. We would never be free that way. And we weren't putting our children through anything. After all, if it was God's will for us, then it was also His will for our children. They were not just overlooked casualties in all of this. If it was God's will for us to have another baby, then He obviously also had a plan for each of our children in it, as well.

After my mom talked to us that day, it seemed like every homily at Mass was about not being afraid to open our hearts and lives to love. By Easter I was pregnant again. Surely God wouldn't ask us to be open to life again and then take the baby away, right?

Throughout my pregnancy, I had a strong feeling that the baby was sick. Whenever I prayed, I had a peace and a sense that God was asking more of me, that there was some way he wanted me to grow through it; however, when I wasn't in prayer, all the fear came rushing back, and I didn't want to believe it.

I began reading a book called *Trustful Surrender to Divine Providence: The Secret of Peace and Happiness* by Father Jean Baptiste Saint-Jure, S.J. and St. Claude de la Colombiere, S.J. It changed my life. The book was not just about accepting God's will, it was about desiring God's will. It was about having your will so completely conformed to God's will that you only desire that. So throughout my pregnancy, as I read this book, I continually prayed that God would conform my heart and my will to His. I realized then that I had never prayed that way with John David.

I also began to research and learn as much as I could about Autosomal Recessive Polycystic Kidney Disease just in case this baby ended up having it too. Through internet research I learned that there had been babies with ARPKD who had survived and were waiting for kidney transplants. Having lost two infants already from ARPKD and always having been told that there is no hope, this came as quite a shock to us. It gave us a new hope that we had never had before. I was also blessed this pregnancy to have a new Ob-Gyn who was a maternal fetal specialist. He watched Jacob's development very closely through ultrasound.

A few years earlier I had started writing journals for each of my children as a way for me to share my heart with them as they were growing up, and then give it to them when they were adults. This one I began when I was pregnant. I have included my journal entries here:

June 14, 2000
(ten weeks pregnant)

My dearest new little one,

You are growing quietly within my womb. I do not know yet if you are a girl or a boy, but I know that I already love you with all my heart, and I always will. Two days ago we saw the doctor. They did an ultrasound and video taped it for us. I came home and watched the video and showed you to your brothers and sister and Grandpa and Grandma Faber. Then Aunt Kathy came over and I showed you to her, too. Seeing you filled me with a flood of emotion. You are so precious, so beautiful! Your little heart was beating strong. You were moving around and I could see outlines of your little face. And I don't even look pregnant yet. Amazing is our God! What an incredible miracle life is. I hope someday you will see this video! I praise God for your life and I pray that you are healthy. I don't want to lose you. I look forward to meeting you and holding you and loving and caring for you for many, many years to come. I love you so much.

September 12, 2000
(twenty-two weeks pregnant)

Dear Jacob,

Yes. We found out by ultrasound that you are a boy, and we have named you Jacob. In Scripture's footnotes, it says that Jacob means "may God protect." We pray that God will protect you now as you develop and keep you free from polycystic kidney disease. I know God has a special and beautiful plan for your life, and I know He will protect you always in whatever way is ultimately best. I have been researching on the internet and am finding out that there is more hope and help for infants with ARPKD. This gives me great hope, because I don't want to lose you. I will have another ultrasound on Thursday to see how you are doing. I want you to know that I love you and will _always_ love you no matter what happens. You are so wonderful. Your life is such a gift. I love you _so_ much, my precious son, Jacob.

September 23, 2000
(twenty-four weeks pregnant)

My dearest baby Jacob,

I fear often for your life. I have ultrasounds often to make sure your kidneys are healthy and functioning properly. If they are not, we will do everything we possibly can to help you. But I need to remember not to worry. Worry and fear only waste the joyful time I have with you now. I don't want to do that. I am thankful for each moment I have with you. I can feel you moving within me more and more each day. It seems like you are growing quite a bit bigger now. I love having you with me. I love you!

I will have another ultrasound in three days. So far you are growing great. I hope that continues. But I place you in the arms of Jesus, for I know and believe with all my heart that His will is always best even when it hurts and we can't understand it. I know that no matter what, Jesus will never leave us and He will carry you and me and our whole family through whatever He asks of us.

For the next several ultrasounds, Jacob showed slight, possible signs of polycystic kidney disease. Although we knew, deep down, this dreaded disease was developing, we held onto hope, as the tests were not completely conclusive. This baby had sufficient fluid for lung development until about thirty-two weeks, so we had hope that maybe he would not have the hypoplastic (brittle) lungs like Nicole and John David. Without the breathing problems, we would have a better chance to address the actual kidney problem.

We spent the remainder of the pregnancy researching and talking with doctors about what could possibly be done after Jacob's birth to help him. The only way that any baby had survived was by doing a complete nephrectomy (removing the baby's enlarged kidneys). Because the polycystic kidneys are so large, the baby's lungs are unable to expand enough to breathe properly. By removing the kidneys, the baby is able to breathe and is put on dialysis until he is strong enough to have a kidney transplant. The survivor I had learned about was six months old and awaiting a transplant. It obviously wouldn't be easy, but it was more hope than we had ever had before.

We met with neonatologists and the kidney specialist in our city and discussed these findings and possibilities for our little Jacob. The plan was for me to be induced on December 18th so that we would have doctors available rather than taking the chance of him being born when many doctors would be gone around Christmas.

Our family and friends from church planned a prayer vigil for us beginning the evening of December 17th (the night of our twelfth wedding anniversary). People signed up for a time slot and prayed in the Chapel before the Blessed Sacrament all through the night and the whole next day and following night, from seven pm, December 17th, until nine am, December 19th.

We felt the prayers, and I ended up going into labor on my own the morning of the 18th, so I did not need to be induced. My labor went smoothly and actually quite quick compared to some of the others. After I was settled in and comfortable from the epidural, my husband and sister ran out quick to get some fast food. They came back to the room with the food, and before they could even eat it, I was ready to push and Jacob was born. Despite having a sufficient amount of fluid for longer, Jacob was still born with the same breathing problems that John David and Nicole had. He was immediately given oxygen and before too long intubated and put on a respirator. He was taken to the NICU, and Father Jim came and baptized him. It was all so familiar. Here we were again. But this time we had a plan and some hope, or so we thought.

To our surprise, while our son lay there fighting for his life, the doctors informed us that they would not be able to remove Jacob's kidneys, because they did not have the means to do dialysis on a newborn infant. We were dumbfounded to be in this situation. After all, we had met with them ahead of time to make sure they would be able to do everything possible for Jacob. If we had known, we would have looked into delivering him somewhere else where they had the means to treat him. Now we were faced with having to transfer Jacob to a children's hospital two-and-a-half hours away. The doctor who was on duty at the time was actually upset that we were going to transfer Jacob. He told us he was going to report on his charts that we had another option. I remember my mom turning to him and asking, "What's that? Let him die?" To which the doctor responded, "Yes." That was not an option for us. We were going to give Jacob every opportunity to live.

On December 19th, Jacob was successfully transported by ambulance to the children's hospital in Ann Arbor, Michigan. The doctors and nurses at the new hospital were amazing and had all the love and expertise to give Jacob the very best care possible. A large team of specialists met immediately and had a plan of action set in place for Jacob's care.

December 21, 2000
(Three days old)

My dear little Jacob,

You were born December 18th, three days ago. You were born with autosomal recessive polycystic kidney disease like your sister, Nicole, and your brother, John David. You are beautiful with blonde hair like your big brother, Michael. You are strong - a real fighter. You are hanging on to life despite many things. Yesterday morning we thought we were going to lose you, but God acted and you climbed uphill a little bit. Yesterday was the feast of St. Jacob. We asked him to intercede for you on his special feast day. I believe God gave us a miracle yesterday and gave us another day with you. You can't believe how happy I was last night to still be sitting at your side and still be with you. What a gift yesterday was. What a gift each minute more I have with you is. Today is a new day and according to doctors we need a big, huge change today. We need another miracle-a complete turnaround. So I again and continually place you in God's hands. And I beg Him and ask all the *angels and saints to plead with Him for an outright miracle of healing for you this day. I do not want to lose you, Jacob. I want to bring you home healthy and whole, raise you, love you, care for you, watch you grow and play and learn. I want you so much. But I have to keep my hope in the Lord and trust that <u>His</u> plan is best, and accept His will over my own and make mine in conformity with His. I do not know what His will is for us today. I pray it is to heal you and allow us to be together. I will be pleading with Him for your life, and we will see how this day unfolds. I love you, my precious son, Jacob Francis. I thank God for every minute with you. You are fearfully and wonderfully made, and I praise God for giving you to me. You are perfect as you are, and I love you and will love you always no matter what. Thank you for enduring this suffering in accordance with God's plan. I am proud of you. I love you.*

I remember those tender, heart-wrenching moments with Jacob, talking to him through my tears. I told him how much I loved him and how much I wanted him to stay with me. I wanted so badly to be able to be his mommy here on this earth. I wanted the opportunity to care for him like only a mother does. Hour upon hour, my husband and I sat at Jacob's side loving him and begging God to heal him. We did the same with Nicole and John David, but this time something was profoundly different. Through prayer and reading the book, *Trustful Surrender to Divine Providence*, God transformed my mind and heart. I had been changed and I firmly believed God's will was best. While I had my own plans and desires, I knew that I needed to trust and continually surrender my will to His. I remember even telling all this to Jacob, that we needed to trust God's will for his life. So while I begged for my will for Jacob's life, I still had to end every prayer with an act of surrender, praying as Jesus did in the garden of Gethsemane, "Your will, not mine, be done." I prayed those words many times at Jacob's side, crying and sobbing, but I meant them, and I trusted...

My dear little Jacob,

When I last wrote, I had no idea that the day held paradise in it for you. The doctors laid it on the line for us. The machines and medications just weren't working. Despite everything they were trying, your oxygen and carbon dioxide would not stay at a level that would make you healthy and sustain life. If it was God's will for you to live, He would have had to make it happen miraculously without the aid of medical science. Later that day we took out all the IV's and took you off the respirator, because it wasn't doing what you needed it to do for you.

I wanted to hold you <u>so</u> much. I hope that before you died you felt some comfort in my arms ... I wanted to hold you forever. It just doesn't seem fair that we only had such a short time together. When I woke up that morning, I had no idea that I would have to say goodbye so soon. I didn't want you to go. I really thought I would take you home someday. I didn't think I was going to have to let you go, and I've missed you so much since then. It's been Christmas and everyone is celebrating. I don't feel like celebrating. I am so tired of trying to be happy, when I feel so sad inside. I just want to be alone and cry.

Today was your burial. I just kept staring at that tiny casket. It's so hard to believe that my baby is in there. Of course, I know that you are not in there. It's just your body. But I kept thinking about your little baby feet and toes and how I used to hold them and caress them when you were in the hospital. I wasn't ready to let you go. I wanted you to stay. I wanted to caress that little baby body and care for you as only a mother does. My heart aches for you. I miss you so much. Please pray for me. I feel like I'm always holding back the tears. Help me not to be afraid to cry even in front of other people or when it doesn't seem like a good time. Please help me to express my feelings and help your brothers and sister to express theirs also.

Jacob died on December 21st, at three days old. Just like that, the fight was over. There we were, once again giving our newborn baby back to Jesus. We had his funeral two days later on December 23rd, and the very next day Michael sang a solo ("Night of Silence") at Christmas Eve Midnight Mass. It was so beautiful. He was so beautiful, and I just kept looking at him, wondering if Jacob would have grown up to look like him. I cannot hear that song to this day without tremendous emotion. We then had Jacob's burial at the cemetery the day after Christmas, which would have been John David's third birthday. It was a very tough Christmas that year, to say the least.

Even though Jacob had died. I still continued to write to him in his journal all the way through my grief. It was a way for me to still "talk" to him and keep him close to me, as well as a sort of prayer journal in which I could write to God.

December 27, 2000
(Six days after your death, and John David's feast day)
Dear Jacob,

I tried to sneak away to my room for a few quiet minutes to think of you and be with you in my heart. Before long Andrea was here, then Ethan. I feel like I need time alone, yet at the same time they all need me too. Pray that Jesus will show me how to meet their needs and my own too. It is so hard. Sometimes it feels impossible. My dear little ones: Trini, Nicole, John David, and Jacob, please pray for us and hold us close during this time and always. Pray that we can help one another and grow closer to God and each other through this time. And please pray for me so I don't feel like I always have to be strong and can never break down. Help me to be humble and rely not on myself, but on God. I love you so much, and I look forward to my homecoming and reunion with you when it is my time to leave this world. Pray unceasingly that none of us, your family, will get lost along the way. Pray that we stay close to God and will all be together in Heaven someday. I love you all so much. You are in my heart forever.

Dear Jacob,

(How I love your name!) I remember being at your side talking with you, praying, crying, and asking, that if you were to go home to Jesus, that you would pray for me so that I never take Michael, Andrea, Seth, and Ethan for granted. Please pray for this for me. I do not want to push them away in my sadness. Pray that Jesus will help me never to complain and help me find the proper balance between the time I need alone to heal and the time I need to embrace them and grieve with them. It is such a gift that Jesus has allowed them to stay here with me, and I don't ever want to take them for granted. Please pray that I will always be faithful to God and be a good wife and mother. I love you, my sweet baby boy, my Saint in Heaven. Hold me close in your heart and prayers, as I will hold you always in my heart. I wish I were holding you now. I miss you so much. When I started this journal, I had hoped to one day give it to you as a way to share my heart with you. Even though you will never read this, I know that through the Communion of Saints you hear me speaking to you as I write. And I know that now, in the Father's presence, you know the depth of my love for you. It will never end. I love you with all my heart.

December 28, 2000
(One week after you entered paradise)

Dear Jacob,

One week ago today I had to say goodbye to you. I know I promised you then that as you dance and sing in Heaven with Jesus and your brothers, Trini and Jack, and your sister, Nicole, I would dance and sing with you with your brothers, Michael, Seth, and Ethan and your sister, Andrea. And I know that someday I will and I will feel deep joy again. But right now, I feel such deep sadness. My heart is filled with sorrow. I am glad that you are rejoicing with the Lord. That is great consolation for me, because that is where I long for all of us to be. For that is what life is all about. But for me right now, in my humanness, to lose you causes such incredible pain and sadness. I know that in time God will heal my broken heart. But for now, please accept my sorrow as a sign of my love and longing for you and please dance and sing for me.

December 30, 2000
(One week after your resurrection Mass)

My precious son Jacob,

One week ago today was the last time I got to see, touch, and kiss your precious newborn baby body. I wanted so much to care for you and watch you grow. I look at Michael and wonder if you would have looked like him. Your hair was like his, and your eyes were a beautiful blue. I wish you could have seen me through those eyes, and I wish I could have looked into those eyes and seen them sparkle when you smiled. I had hoped to have many, many years with you. Not having you leaves such an emptiness within me. I miss you so much. I am so thankful, though, for the time I had with you. Those hours sitting at your side caressing your little baby body, beautiful soft skin, tiny toes and fingers, crying with you, talking and praying with you - those are moments I will treasure forever. No words could ever express the tenderness of those moments. Just being with you gave me strength. I could look at you and know that I would do anything for you. I would do it all over and over again for you, in order that you could have life. Such love overwhelmed me for you. My heart was open wide to you and to God's plan for you and all of us. Love overflowed for you. Tears overflowed for you. I wanted you so bad, yet I knew that *true joy and peace could only be found in God's will. And when I was with you, I could cry and pray confidently for God's will. I am happy for you now - for you understand all things and have complete joy in God's presence. There is nothing greater I could wish for you. But as for me, I am filled with sorrow because my heart aches for you. I wanted more time with you. I wanted to bring you home with me. I wanted God to heal you and show us how to beat this disease. When it became obvious that the doctors had exhausted all resources and nothing was helping, I hope we did all that we should have. I felt bad having you lying there suffering when all that equipment wasn't helping you. I felt God was calling you home to paradise. I just hope we didn't rush it. I want only to do God's will and want only to have loved you as God would have me. Yet I feel uneasy about it. Please, little Jacob, pray to Jesus for me that He will give me peace about this. Pray that I can let you go and be at peace that this was all God's plan for you. Pray that God will heal me and reconcile me in every way that is needed and give me peace and acceptance of the way I mothered and loved you while I could. Please forgive me for all the worry during pregnancy and if I didn't bond with you as deeply as I should have. Forgive me if I did anything that hurt you and did not care for you and love you as I should have. I do not want to hurt you in any way. Pray for me that I will never take for granted the gift of being a mother and wife. Please pray that my will be conformed to God's and that I will always be a faithful and loving wife and mother and daughter of the King. I love you, my Jacob, and I am thankful for your life and all my Saints in Heaven. With your intercession and God's grace, I will make it through. I love you and always will. Thank you for still being with me.*

As this entry shows, along with my grief, I went through a period of guilt, wondering and worrying if I had done all that I could and should have done for Jacob. I suppose I went through it in one way or another with each of my babies who died. My heart ached so much for them, and I just didn't want to have hurt them in any way. I have learned that feeling guilt is a very normal part of grief, even if there is realistically nothing to feel guilty about.

Dear Jacob,

It is so hard to believe that you are gone. In my mind I am having a hard time letting you go. At the time I just did what I felt I had to do. I accepted the inevitable. But now it is so hard to accept. Did I have to let you go so soon? At the time, I felt so bad for making you suffer any longer when the machines were not giving us any hope. <u>God</u> would have to have acted to heal you with or without the machines. I think I just don't want to accept that you are gone. I don't want to have to let you go. Every time, the finality of death is so hard to accept. You are gone and there is nothing, absolutely nothing I can do to bring you back. I will never hold you as an infant again. I will never get to mother you and teach you and hug and kiss you. You will never need me like a baby needs his mother. I will not be your source of comfort or look into your eyes or hear you say "mama." It is just so hard to believe you are gone. I wasn't prepared to have you die or even to let you die. I prepared myself for the long haul. I really thought you were going to live. I was convinced that I was going to bring you home, here, someday. Help me to be able to accept that I had to let you go. Help me to know beyond a shadow of a doubt that God's will was done and help me to accept it. But at the same time, please stay alive in my heart. I don't ever want to forget the time we had together and the preciousness of it. I'm so afraid of having the memories dull or fade in my mind. I don't ever want to forget how you looked and how I felt when I was with you. I don't want to forget your little face or your little feet and toes that I spent so much time caressing. I don't want to forget how tiny and how good your little hand felt in mine up on my shoulder when I held you. Little Jacob, I love you so much, and I just don't want to let you go. I know I already did, and I would again and again if God asked me to. But it's just so hard to accept in my mind and heart because I want you here with me so bad, and I planned on bringing you home. Pray for me that I can accept your death, but also keep your memory alive in my heart forever.

Jesus, hear my thoughts and my heart. Heal my broken heart and help me to deal with the letting go in Your light and Your way. I know You are with me and Jacob is too. I love You so much, and I thank You for Jacob's life. He is a gift. I love him so much. Bring to completion all You have started through his life and help us all to grow in acceptance of Your will over our own.   I love you sweet baby Jacob. Pray for us now.

January 9, 2001
(Three weeks after our trip to Ann Arbor)

Dear Jacob,

I am sitting in the Eucharistic Chapel right now. The last time I was here, you were with me. It was the night before you were born. I was filled with fear but also great hope. Now as I sit here, the fear is gone and the hope is gone. For my hope was that you would live, and that I would bring you home to our house someday, and that we would have many years together on this earth - that I would be able to care for you as your mother, holding you, comforting you, protecting you, teaching you. And that love was going to be very consuming because of your kidney disease. My life would be different with you, little Jacob, my son. So it is so hard to sit here now without you and so hard to believe you are gone - the fight, the struggle for your life here is over. How can that be? It was way too short. I wanted and hoped for much more time with you.

As time passes, the tears come less frequently, the pictures in my mind are less vivid. The feeling of those hours with you are less intense, and I hate it. I feel like I am losing you all over again. I'm not ready for my time with you to be over. Please stay alive forever in my heart and memories. Help me to feel the strength and faith and love for you that I felt when I was with you - and the desire to do only God's will. I couldn't look at you and desire anything other than what God desired for you, because that's what is best and where we find peace. I want to feel you with me. Help me. Help me. Pray for me that I can hold on to you in the ways I should and that I can also let go as I should. Help me not to be afraid. Help me to accept God's healing, peace and joy at the proper times. I love you so much, and I long for you, my baby boy.

Pray also Jacob for the many people who came to this Chapel day and night and prayed for us. Pray that God be close to them, and pray that they be touched and changed and brought closer to God through your life.

Thank You, Jesus, for the outpouring of love for us from this Parish. I still am amazed that they did what they did for us. Bless them. Thank You for them - for the support of this Parish.

A few times I made reference to how I felt when I was with Jacob. Throughout my pregnancy, my heart and mind were transformed, and I truly tried to turn my will over to God. When I was in prayer during the pregnancy, or by Jacob's side after his birth, I felt so much strength and so much longing to do God's will and trust him completely. It is hard to explain, but I could not end a prayer without asking for His will, not mine, to be done. This was so different from how I was with John David, begging and pleading for my own will with no acceptance of God's plan.

After Jacob died, though, I felt like I had done God's will and that was that. It was over, and I was just left alone to pick up the pieces and try to heal and move on. I didn't necessarily want to move on. I was afraid to let go of the pain. I was afraid that in letting go of the pain, I would lose Jacob. I didn't want to forget the tender moments I spent with him and all the strength and trust in God that I had felt. I wanted to hang on to him and remember always the strong resolve I had to do God's will, but I felt a bit abandoned by God. One night when I was all alone in our family room, I spoke out loud to God saying, "Lord, You asked me to open my heart to love again, and I did. Then You asked me to give Jacob back to You, and I did. I did Your will, now where are You? You've left me all alone." In that moment I felt God's presence with me, and I felt Him say to me, "Oh no Chris, I am with you, and I have a plan for you right now in the middle of your pain and grief."

January 10, 2001

My dear little Jacob,

God is so good to me. Thank you for loving me and praying for me. Thank you for staying with me. I have new hope today. For God has shown me that I will not lose you in the healing. You are not in the pain and sorrow. You are with Jesus and in doing God's will is where I will feel, experience, and hold on to you. God has let me know that He has a plan for me now, even in my pain and emptiness. This is not just something to get through. This is all still part of His plan, and I need to keep seeking His will every day and grow through this and seek God's will for my children and how God wants me to help them grow through it. And for a brief moment, in realizing God had a plan for me even now and that I needed and desired to fulfill His will, for a brief moment, I felt you with me, and I felt all the strength and faith and grace and even joy that I felt when I was with you.

Thank You, Jesus, for such a wonderful gift. You truly answered my prayer and heard my cries to You for help. Please help me to seek You every day. Keep me in Your will. For in Your will is where I find peace and *strength and yes, even joy in the <u>midst of great sorrow</u>, and in doing Your will is where I will always find Jacob, <u>alive</u>! I love You, Jesus. I love you, Jacob. Thank you both for hearing my cries. Thank you for staying with me. I love you so much. Jacob, help me to keep my eyes on the goal and know that we will be together forever in perfect joy in Heaven. It is hard for me to even comprehend that, but I know that if I keep my eyes on Jesus, He will give me the grace to hold you and ponder you and God's glory in my heart until I see you both face to face.*

From this day on, something amazingly beautiful and miraculous began to take place in me. Right in the midst of my pain and grief, I began to experience a joy I had never known before. In the midst of my loss, God's plan looked so beautiful and perfect. I can't even tell you why, but I felt so privileged and blessed by everything that had happened. It was an experience I can't adequately explain. I just continued to journal through it:

January 12, 2001

My dear little Jacob,

I think I am experiencing just a tiny inkling of the joy you are now living in. God has blessed me with a peace and deep joy beyond human comprehension. I just want to cry. But not tears of sorrow, rather tears of joy and tears of gratitude. I feel so blessed by your life and so blessed that God has called me to be a part of His plan for you and through you. I feel so blessed to have been chosen for this and so blessed by the love that God just lavishes on me. Even sorrow and sacrifice have joy in the light of God's plan and the acceptance of His will and conformity of our will to His. Jacob, I love you so much, and I am filled with joy and gratitude for your life. God has blessed my life with you and the opportunity to carry you within me, give birth to you, suffer and hope with you, and love you with all my heart. I feel like I'm on a honeymoon with Jesus. I feel His love so strongly. There is so much delight in His will if only we open our hearts to it. Pray that I will not forget this, and that I will continually give my will over to Jesus and conform my will totally to His. Help me to use the gifts Jesus has given me to help others. Help me not to get so busy with daily life that I do not take the time to seek Jesus and His will for my life and our family every day. Pray that we all continue to grow closer to Jesus and that my will be conformed to God's will in the little things, shocking things, painful things, and even huge tragedies-everything. Pray that I can give all of you children, daddy and all those I love to the Lord in everything and cling to the Lord in everything, conforming my will to his in _everything_. This is where true joy is, and I know this is where you are too. I love you, Jacob. I am privileged to be your mother. I am and always will be grateful for you in my life.

January 19, 2001

My dear little Jacob,

When Jesus revealed to me that He had a plan for me even now in the midst of grief, I had no idea what a gift He had for me - what a plan He has for me. It has been amazing how He is transforming my mind and heart and how He is filling me. The healing God has for me is beyond what I could have imagined. I feel God is strengthening me in all ways and bringing me closer to Him and to you and Trini, Nicole, and John David. I even can begin to imagine you as an adult, as the person, the man of God that you are, and this image of you and Trini, Nicole, and John David this way is actually comforting to me. This is amazing. I've never been able to picture any of you this way. It was so hard to let go of you as my babies. Yet now I feel so close to you all and feel so much love for you as the beautiful people, Saints, that you are. I missed you as my baby. I wanted to mother and take care of you, but now I feel like you are caring for me, and I am growing so close to you and loving the person you *are, not just the little baby body through which you came into being and were given to me. I love you so much, and I can't thank Jesus enough for the ways He is healing me and making Himself so present to me. I had no idea of the greatness and beauty of His plan. Please praise and thank Him always for me.*

For about two weeks, I had an experience of God and Jacob that was as real as anything I have ever known or experienced in my life. There was a depth and peace and joy beyond anything I could have imagined. There was healing more complete than I ever thought possible. I felt God with me. I felt Jacob with me. I actually felt as if I knew Jacob more completely than my living children. The veil between Heaven and earth was very thin. It was a supernatural experience, and wow, was it amazing beyond words. I believe it was a glimpse of Heaven, and it left me forever changed. I always felt like a wounded and broken person after the deaths of my babies. Each new living baby filled my broken heart with great joy and brought healing, but inside I always still felt deeply scarred. I thought that was just my new normal. But this time, God took away all the brokenness and made me more whole than I had ever been, right in the midst of the grief.

January 27, 2001

My dearest Jacob,

The last couple of weeks have been so amazing. It was even hard for me to be sad at your loss, because I didn't feel like I lost you. It actually was as if I knew you more and, in a way, <u>deeper</u> than how I am able to know my babies or children on earth. God let me see and experience and know you as the person and Saint you are in Heaven. I could hardly look at pictures of you in your earthly baby body and see you as the same person or even miss you, because your life was so alive and present to me in this deeper, spiritual way. This time has been an extraordinary and *supernatural experience and gift. I feel God has given me a glimpse of who you are, and also Trini, Nicole, and John David, and a small taste of the love and relationship we will share in Heaven as Saints of God. What a true <u>homecoming</u> it will be!! I have experienced an overwhelming love and joy and relationship like never before. Through this experience I feel God has completely healed me from <u>all</u> the losses I have endured and made me whole once again.*

The sadness has begun to return over the last few days, but it feels okay and natural. I thank God for the supernatural experience and the ways He has healed me, changed me, and given me new hope through it - through you. Please pray that I will continue always to seek God's will and ways I can grow and help the children to grow through each and every day. I don't want to waste a day just getting through it. I want God to work in me, change me, and help me grow closer to Him, in and through each and every day. Help me to seek Him and offer all to Him. This week, though busy and overwhelming, is His - not mine. Help me to seek Him, do His will, and grow through it.

I love you, my precious baby, my Saint of God. Stay close to me. Pray for your daddy and brothers and sister. And praise God always for the many gifts and blessings He has given me. I am so grateful.

God had blessed me with a peace and joy in the middle of my pain that humanly made no sense. I can only describe it by using Philippians 4:7 where it talks about "the peace of God which surpasses all understanding." That is truly what God gave me. It was so beautiful, but after about two weeks, this glimpse of Heaven began to fade away. My mom told me later that she had been praying for me all along, because she knew that what I was experiencing was a supernatural gift from God, and that I would eventually have to return to the natural, physical world again.

Dear Jacob,

As time goes on, I am left in the natural, human world once again. I know I am forever changed. I know God's will and plan is perfect, but it was amazing to truly experience that for a while. It wasn't just head knowledge. I truly experienced it - a joy and total delight in God's plan. I couldn't even wish for you to have lived or for anything to be different. Everything was <u>perfectly</u> beautiful just as God planned it. Even the hardships didn't seem hard - there was only joy - an unreal and supernatural joy. Even in a store if I saw baby things, I'd start to feel sad and then when I thought of God and the beauty of His plan, all sadness was <u>overcome</u> by complete joy.

I no longer experience these supernatural feelings, and sometimes it's even hard to imagine that I felt them so strongly and powerfully. It was all so amazing and humanly unreal. It was such a gift - a taste of Heaven. Pray for us that we stay close to God and will be with you in Heaven someday.

Daddy was also blessed. He told me that at your funeral, he felt great joy. I know he was experiencing God. I could see it in his eyes. I thank Jesus for letting Daddy experience Him so profoundly. And I thank God for letting this experience last so long for me, not just a brief moment. Pray for us that, even though we can't always experience God's ways so profoundly, we will always stay faithful.

I do still feel a sense of peace when I am reminded that God is close to me and has a purpose and plan in each and every day, even really busy ones like today. I give this day to Him, and I ask you, Jacob, my son, my dear Saint, to pray for me that I'll stay loving and peaceful today and fulfill His purpose for me this day. And pray that each child and all those I'm around feel God's love through me this day.

February 1, 2001

Dear Jacob,

I am realizing more and more what a rare and special gift I was given. During that blessed time when God allowed me to experience and feel things as they really are in Heaven, I couldn't even see your loss as a hardship or cross. It only was a blessing and privilege. At that time having you in my arms could not have filled me with more joy than the beauty of God's plan. It was absolutely perfect and <u>so</u> beautiful. I don't even know why - <u>I just</u> <u>know</u> <u>that</u> <u>nothing</u> <u>else</u> <u>could</u> <u>have filled</u> <u>me</u> <u>with</u> <u>more joy.</u>

*Now that this experience is gone, I can't imagine how I could have felt this way. It seems so unreal, almost insensitive. I am realizing what an amazing gift it was and what a miracle! I asked God for a miracle. Well, He gave me one - one that allowed me to experience things <u>**so different**</u> from the human experience. I wish I could experience it forever - I guess that's what Heaven is like. I have great hope now for eternity. But for now, it is so hard to live in the purely human. I miss you. My heart is saddened and lonely for you. Your grandpa and grandma are coming from California today. They planned the trip to come see <u>you.</u> Aunt Mickie and Uncle Greg are coming, too. They were coming to be your godparents. We were going to have your baptism this weekend. I <u>know</u> beyond a shadow of a doubt that God's plan is best. But I don't <u>feel</u> it anymore. I have to walk by faith now. What a rare and extraordinary gift God gave me. What a loving Father He is. Pray for me now, as I must once again embrace His holy darkness. I love you.*

Through our experiences of having and losing our children, Chris and I have related strongly to and drawn strength from the words of the song "Holy Darkness" by Dan Schutte. Most of the time we cannot even begin to understand God's plan for our lives. So we must trust what we cannot see and embrace His holy Darkness.

"Holy Darkness"

Holy darkness, blessed night,
Heaven's answer hidden from our sight.
As we await You, O God of silence,
We embrace Your holy night.

I have tried you in fires of affliction;
I have taught your soul to grieve.
In the barren soil of your loneliness,
There will I plant my seed.

I have taught you the price of compassion;
You have stood before the grave.
Though My love can seem like a raging storm,
This is the love that saves.

In your deepest hour of darkness
I will give you wealth untold.
When the silence stills your spirit,
Will My riches fill your soul.

March 1, 2001

Dear Jacob,

It seems like it has been so long since I've written to you. I miss you. We've had so much company lately that I feel like I haven't had much time to "be with you" in my mind and heart. I haven't had much personal prayer lately either. I think that's part of the reason I haven't been able to feel you lately. I know you are with Jesus, and when I'm in union with Him and seeking His will, I will experience His love and graces. And where He is, you are also. I long to feel Jesus and you with me.

Help me to take time to seek Jesus every day. Help me to keep my focus centered on Jesus and doing His will. I miss you and my heart aches and becomes saddened for you when I don't take time to be with Jesus and you. I wanted to keep you here so much, but I know true joy is in total conformity to God's will, and deep in my heart, I know I desire to be conformed to God's will more than anything. Help me to keep my sight on that. It is so easy to become blinded and confused. Help me to keep my eyes on the goal. I love you, sweetheart. I thank Jesus for you.

March 6, 2001

Dear Jacob,

Yesterday I received your autopsy report in the mail. I didn't realize it would affect me the way it did. It was so hard. Just opening the envelope, I was uptight. My heart started pounding and my breathing seemed harder. I felt sick and shaky inside. Then, as I read it, it seemed so awful. I had read and studied while you were alive with the purpose of trying to help you. And now, here I am studying you. It doesn't seem right. It's not the way I wanted it to be. For a while I could see things so clearly, "through Heaven's eyes," as you can see them. There was no sadness or fear there. Everything looked--and was--so perfect and beautiful. Now I feel blind. Daddy and I were talking last night, and we are both filled with fear to have more children now. It is too hard to love and hope and dream with you, our children, and then have to let you go so soon. When I have you with me, I know that no matter the pain, I would do it all a hundred times over for you. But then when I am left alone without you, I so easily become filled with fear. Why can't we always see as God sees? Why do we become so blind and afraid? Pray that God will heal us and help us and keep our hearts fully open to Him. Pray that He will show us and guide us when He wants to bless us with another child, if He does. And please pray that He will fill us with peace and even joy, not fear. Help us to let go of our fears and trust in the beauty and perfection of God's plans even when we do not and cannot see clearly. Pray that I may grow in perfect surrender and conformity to God's will. That is where peace and joy can always be found.

I miss you, Jacob. I used to bless you in my tummy at night before bed. Now at night when I bless the kids, I always feel like I missed someone. It's you - I miss you. I love you, dear Jacob, with all my heart.

Although God had blessed me so much, and shown me so clearly that His will is beautiful and perfect even when I can't understand it, I am still so weak and human and my emotions were all over the place. I truly believed that God's will was best, but it still hurt at times. I had many moments of great pain and sadness, but I was also blessed with moments of great grace and peace. God continued to bless me and show me that He was always with me.

March 15, 2001

My dear Jacob,

It's hard to believe that it has been almost three months since you were born. Time stops for no one and seems to go faster and faster. It is so weird right now: sometimes when I look at your pictures, everything seems so unreal - almost like none of it ever happened. God has given me so much peace and contentment right now. It seems almost unimaginable that I could carry you within me for eight months, give birth to you, hope and pray with you, long for you, desire you so much, hold you in my arms, feel your body against mine, cuddle and kiss you, then have to let you go, and yet I am okay. That seems so surreal; it doesn't make sense. I know it is the power of God's grace and healing. I don't feel a great desire and need to have another baby in order to fill the emptiness from your loss and bring more complete healing and a more full joy back into my heart and life. It is so different this time than the other times. I feel rather a longing to do God's will, to be completely conformed to His will, and to be freed from my fear of losing people I love and even of my own death. God helped me walk with Him and seek _His_ will throughout your life and death, and He has filled me with such peace, contentment, and complete healing. Humanly, it all seems so unimaginable, so inhuman and unreal, yet _He_ has done it. He is amazing and so good to me, almost too good at times. Sometimes I wish I could feel more sadness from your loss. Why? I don't really know. Sometimes it just doesn't seem right to be okay in the face of it all. Yet, I believe this is God's way - God's grace, God's love, God's perfect healing, and God's perfect plan. I thank God for you and the beautiful gift you are. And I _know_ that it did all happen, and that you are _so_ _very_ _alive_ and well. And I await the day when we will be together again. I love you, Jacob! I love you, God, my Father!

April 11, 2001

Dear Jacob,

It is Holy Week now. Tomorrow will be Holy Thursday, and we will begin the Triduum. This week makes me think of you. I believe you were conceived during Holy Week (Good Friday) last year. Then began our journey together. I love you so much and am grateful that God gave you to me. I feel so much like I know you and you are with me, even though you are not here physically. I am so thankful for the relationship God has given us. It is such a tremendous blessing. I am truly experiencing the Communion of Saints with you. What a gift, and what a gift you are! I have lost you physically as an infant, but I have not lost you. You are _so_ _very_ _very_ alive, and you are so very close to me. I thank Jesus for allowing this and allowing me to know and experience you. You are so beautiful, so perfect. I feel close to God when I think of you. I know you are with God, and you are a beautiful Saint of God. Please pray for me that I can experience how alive Trini, Nicole, and John David are now also. I want to feel them too and know them like I feel I know you. But no matter the feelings, I _know_ they are alive and Saints of God just as you are, and I will accept however God wishes our relationship to be at this time. I know you are all loving us and praying for us, and I look forward to being _fully_ together in Heaven. I love you all with all my heart, with a mother's love, for you are my children. I am grateful to be your mother, even though I did not get to be your mommy here on earth.

April 22, 2001
(One week after Easter)

Dear Jacob,

I thank Jesus, and I thank you, for you are still so very present to me. I hope it will always be this way. You are so much a part of my life. It's different though. I don't often think of you as my baby. Rather, I think of you and feel your presence as my son, a holy man of God. When I write this, I get tears in my eyes. Why? I'm not sure. Maybe just because you are so beautiful and because it is so incredibly beautiful to experience you as God does - to see through Heaven's eyes.

It is so amazing how when you were here on earth, you could not speak or understand anything. You had no human knowledge, yet your soul was full and pure and yearning for the Lord. And now in Heaven you are perfectly and completely fulfilled and understand all things more clearly than I can possibly imagine. We tend to get so caught up in the body and our accomplishments and so easily forget about the soul within that only longs for Christ and that will only find fulfillment in Christ. On Holy Thursday, Father Jim talked about how we need to care for each other's journey of the soul. This is what is truly important. When I go to receive Communion and I am holding Ethan, my heart is flooded

- 67 -

with emotion when Father Jim places his hand on Ethan and says, "may Jesus be alive in your heart." It confirms in me once more that my true heart's desire for him and all of us is that we always be close to Jesus and do His will, no matter what it requires. The only way we'll find true peace and joy is in total conformity to God's will. You have won the crown, Jacob. Yes, I miss having you here as my baby, but what I truly desire for you is what you have - eternal life with Jesus. For in His presence is fullness of joy. Pray for us that we can remember always that this is what is important and that the journey of our souls is our major responsibility.

The Lord has blessed me so much with you and through you. God is opening my eyes. I feel so close to God the Father now. Before, I had a hard time relating to God, the Father. I thought mostly of Jesus. I also feel God has transformed my heart. I always knew that I should desire God's will because it was somehow what was best, but I wanted it because I knew I should, not because I truly desired it. Now, I feel I truly desire only God's will. I get distracted sometimes, but deep in my heart I know that His will and being wholly conformed to it is my true heart's desire. There is where my soul is at rest, even in the midst of suffering. I love Jesus so much and God the Father, and I thank and praise Him for His presence in my life, heart, and soul. I will be forever grateful for the journey of soul I have taken with you. I see things so differently now. Pray that I do not become distracted and my vision clouded. Pray that I will always be conformed to God's will and be attentive to others' journey of the soul.

At Easter, during the Triduum liturgies, I was able to envision all four of you, my children in Heaven, as beautiful Saints of Heaven a couple of times. Though only momentary, I experienced great joy in this, in all of you, in God's perfect plan, in the beauty of your souls and your true fulfillment in God's presence. God, You are an awesome God. In _Your_ *presence is fullness of joy - for each of us. Please Lord, let none of us be lost.*

As the months passed, I realized more and more how special and extraordinary my experience with Jacob had been. Being weak and human, I needed and still need to constantly remind myself of the joy that comes through surrender. I quickly try to take back control and allow myself to fear many things. How thankful I am that I journaled through my experience of grief, so I can continually be reminded to trust and surrender my will to God's. This is why I want to share my experience: as I wrote at the beginning of this story, that which I feared ended up filling my life with a new hope and a new joy. I hope and pray that when you face difficult circumstances or decisions, you may find the grace and courage to trust God and surrender your life completely to Him.

May 6, 2001
(I love you, dear Jacob)

Dear Jacob,

Last Sunday was First Communion at St. Thomas. It made me think a lot about you. Last year on the day of First Communion is when I found out I was pregnant with you. Everything we went through with you is what we feared and a lot of the reason we were afraid to conceive another child. Yet, here it is a year later and even though we lost you and had to face our fears, I don't, even for a second, wish that you had never been conceived. I am thankful for you and for this journey of faith I have made with you and Jesus this past year. Jesus gave me a rare and supernatural gift and has allowed me to know your soul. Though you came as an infant, knowing nothing, within a few days your soul had reached its full potential - perfection, absolute joy and peace. And what God is showing me now is that in the very same way, each of us has a soul that will only reach fulfillment in Heaven with Christ. No matter our personalities, ailments, limitations, sins, likes, dislikes, strengths, or weaknesses, the essence of who we are--our souls--will only find fulfillment and joy in Heaven with God. Nothing else will bring us to fulfillment, true joy and peace. For example, even though Seth acts rough and tough and doesn't always seem interested in God, while Michael from a very young age showed incredible love for God and deep faith, they both will only find true joy and fulfillment in Christ. And what they seek, whether they know it or not, is Jesus. The same goes for the hardened criminal, the homeless, the rich, the famous, etc. The beauty and perfection I see in you, Jacob, is the hidden potential and longing within each person. Pray dear Jacob that we will care for the journey of the soul of each individual.

June 1, 2001

Dear Jacob,

What is it like to die? You experienced birth and death back-to-back. I wonder if they are similar. After all, death is just rebirth-birth into eternal life. And eternal life is what we long for. It is our goal. So why then do we fear death so much? It seems like we look on death as tragedy and most of our prayers center on our health and protecting people from death. Yes, we need to protect life, but I don't think we should fear death so much. Pray for us, Jacob, that we will await our birth unto eternal life with great joy. Jesus, please help us to prepare with longing and joy for this rebirth. Help us to help our children in this, too, and not fill them with a sense of fear about death. Help us to truly cling to You and not this world. Prepare us for this new birth and help us be ready and willing to let others go when it is their time of new birth. For, as Saint Francis of Assisi said, "it is in dying that we are born to eternal life." Isn't this what life is really all about?

Blessed be the God and Father of our Lord Jesus Christ, who in His great mercy gave us a new birth to a living hope through the resurrection of Jesus Christ from the dead, to an inheritance that is imperishable, undefiled, and unfading, kept in heaven for you who by the power of God are safeguarded through faith, to a salvation that is ready to be revealed in the final time. In this you rejoice, though now for a little while you may have to suffer through various trials, so that the genuineness of your faith, more precious than gold that is perishable even though tested by fire, may prove to be for praise, glory, and honor at the revelation of Jesus Christ. Although you have not seen Him you love Him; even though you do not see Him now yet believe in Him, you rejoice with an indescribable and glorious joy, as you attain the goal of your faith, the salvation of your souls." (1 Peter 1:3-9)

*Help us keep our hearts set on the goal, salvation - for <u>all</u>. And help us not to get distracted by our earthly desires. Form our hearts that we truly desire and <u>long for **You**</u>.*

July 29, 2001

Dear Jacob,

It has been almost two months since I have written - and I sure can feel it too. My prayer life also has been lacking, and when I feel far from God, I feel far from you, too. I want to keep my mind and heart conformed to doing God's will. That is where true peace and joy are. God fills me with peace and joy, even in the cross. I just sometimes get busy and don't seek Him. We have been on vacation the past few weeks. I have had a lot of fun, but I have missed you so much more. Every little baby I see makes me desire you. I have been starting to feel a deep longing to have another baby, but I don't want to conceive just because I _want_ a baby or just to fulfill my desires. I want to have another baby in total conformity to God's will. I have to find joy in having another baby not because I'm excited to have and hold, love and raise them. My joy must come in loving them and caring for them while I may and allowing God's purpose and perfect plan for their lives to be fulfilled, no matter how long or short that may be. I must cooperate with and be in conformity with God's holy plan and will - not my own will and desire. I want my only desire to be doing God's will. This is where true joy and peace and love for another person lie. Many people comment and say that we are so brave to go through what we have with you and Trini and Nicole and John David. But you know, when you were dying, there was nothing we could do about it. We had no choice but to deal with it and accept it. I feel the Lord is telling me that in any future pregnancies the bravery would be to openly accept whatever God's will is for each child, even in the midst of fear and not knowing whether my baby will be healthy and live or not. Most pregnancies I have walked through with great fear and begging for the baby not to have ARPKD. It was clear that my joy would come when I knew they were healthy and I held them in my arms. Now God is calling me to have joy in the midst of uncertainty - joy in simply doing God's will, no matter what that means - joy in the beauty of life and God's plan for each and every human being - total conformity to the will and plan of God in my life and the lives of those around me, especially you, my children.

Dearest Jacob, pray for me and Daddy that we can live this way and accept new life this way. Pray that God gives us direction and peace in every aspect of our lives and that our desires would truly be conformed to God's will. Help us to spend our lives for good and use the gifts God has given us. I will forever be grateful for your life, dear Jacob. God has *changed me through you. You are a true gift - a true Saint. You bring me always closer to God.*

Father, I love You. Your plan is perfectly beautiful. Thank You for sharing Your son, Jacob, with me.

August 5, 2001

My dear little Jacob,

We have just returned home from a Charismatic Conference. I know that you were there with me. I was very blessed by the songs and praise and worship. It was beautiful to be there with Daddy and the kids, and on both nights, I felt I was praising with all of you children. I know you and Trini and Nicole and John David were there, standing right beside us praising God. I sensed your presence <u>so</u> strongly and tears of joy flowed for love of you, all my children, and Jesus, and love and joy in God's most perfect and beautiful plan for us. I remember in the past, being at conferences and feeling joy in God, but also very broken and wounded because of the pain of losing my precious babies. This time I felt so whole, so free from burden and pain, so privileged and blessed by God. I felt no brokenness or even like any of this was a cross. Rather, I felt so privileged to be a part of God's plan in this way. I felt so complete and loved by God. I know, Jacob, that through and with you, I touched Heaven. I experienced Heaven - at least a glimpse of it. And the beauty and perfection of God's will is still so vivid in my mind. I was in the midst of great sorrow and yet there was no pain - only perfect joy. It has changed me and how I look at God's call for my life.

This weekend, Father Graham kept talking about going deeper into our relationship with Christ. It is just hard to imagine even more intimacy with Christ than what He has already shown me and blessed me with in this past year with you. It has been so incredible, miraculous, and beautiful. Yet, as the weekend went on, there seemed to be just one small

- 73 -

frustration or disappointment after another. And my attitude changed. I became uptight that things weren't going as planned. So now it is clear that my step deeper must be to surrender <u>all</u> my plans, even the little ones, and accept the happenings of each and every day as God's will for that moment in my life - even all the little inconveniences and frustrations. God is in control - not me. He knows what we need. My will must be <u>completely</u> conformed to His - right down to the smallest of details. I started the weekend trying to be positive and accept it all as God's will. But by the end, I had failed in many ways. Pray dear Jacob that I will grow in this and not be selfish, wanting things to always go my way. Help me to truly trust and surrender <u>all</u> to the Lord, <u>at all times</u>. I love you Jacob, my Saint of God, and I love You, dear Jesus, and thank You for Your unfailing love and the many, many blessings in my life.

September 9, 2001

My dearest Jacob,

I had been thinking for the past couple of weeks that maybe I was pregnant, but today I realized I am not. I didn't realize just how much I was hoping I was. I have been so, so sad today. I feel empty and depressed and I have an ache deep within my heart. It hurts so much. It makes me realize how much I miss you and how I long to hold and care for a baby as only a mother can. The thought of waiting seems almost unbearable. It's confusing because I know God has given me this desire and it's beautiful, but at the same time I don't want it to be a selfish desire. I need to be fully conformed to God's will, no matter what it means. In God's will is where there is perfect joy, even when we do not understand, and often we don't. But I must embrace His holy darkness <u>always</u>. I don't always have to understand; I don't always have to <u>feel</u> joy. I need only to **accept** and allow God to fill me and delight my heart [in His ways] . . .

Dear Jesus,

*I feel so broken-hearted today, but I don't have great reason to. I can think of others like Mom whose heart is so heavily burdened right now and Mom and Uncle Don's friend who just lost his wife. They are suffering and broken now. So I take this heaviness and heartache I feel, and I offer it up for them. If I can carry it now in order to relieve some of their pain, then I accept it and offer it up for them. I do not just want to wallow in my own selfishness and desire. Take my desire to care for and mother another baby and use it for good to ease the pain of others. I give it to You. Help me to truly surrender all to You and desire **only** Your will - desire **only** to serve You, Lord. I love You, Jesus. I love you, Jacob. I miss you.*

I realize that in this journal I say over and over again that I need to be completely conformed to God's will, and that in God's will is where there is perfect joy. I really wasn't trying to preach it to anyone but myself. As I journaled and prayed and encountered crosses, I had to keep reminding myself. I am so weak that even after all God did for me and allowed me to experience, I still continued to struggle with letting go of my own will and trusting His in each new circumstance. I had to keep reminding myself and praying for the grace and strength to surrender.

September 15, 2001

Dear Jacob,

I have a deep longing in my heart for a baby right now. I went to a baby shower today and felt saddened. I don't want to be selfish and focus on my desires. I want my desire to be God's will. There is also so much going on in our country [9/11] and the world right now that is sad and frightening. Help me to use all my varied emotions of fear, depression, sadness, longing, confusion, etc. somehow for good. Help me not to get caught up in my emotions, but rather offer them all up for *good and carry them as a way of relieving someone else and offering them all as a sacrifice of prayer. Let my heart be formed as the heart of God is. Help me to desire only God's holy and perfect will. I love you, son. I love You, Jesus. Help me to keep my eyes and heart on **You always**.*

In many ways, my journal to Jacob had become my prayer journal. I would start out talking to Jacob about what I was feeling or going through, and usually end up in prayer. Since Jacob is always in Jesus' presence, I was constantly asking him to pray for me, and my journaling always seemed to lead me to Jesus.

September 23, 2001

Dear Jacob,

Lately I've been really struggling with keeping my focus on Jesus and not giving in to worry. Through you, God showed me the absolute beauty of His plan even when it didn't humanly look beautiful. I know that true peace and joy are in total conformity to God's will. Lately I feel like I am fighting that and seeking my own will instead of God's. I have been so worried about Michael with the constant headache he has. We've been to the pediatrician, the eye doctor, the chiropractor two times, and the dentist to get a bite splint to relax his jaw. We've tried six different medications, and yet nothing is taking away his headache. Now I am getting worried that it could be something serious. I am scared, and my stomach immediately goes into knots the minute I think about it. I have no peace and experience no joy or comfort in desiring to do only God's will. Last night at Mass, I felt all this too and couldn't possibly imagine how I could handle it and find any peace in accepting God's will if it is something bad. But then for a brief moment it was all clear, and I felt no worry. I felt grace and peace, and I knew it would be alright. I knew God was with me and His plan was perfect. Then, as quickly as that peace came, it left. Jacob, please pray for me that I can live in that peace and cling to God and be conformed to His holy will. I know He can do that. He did it for me with you, and whenever I went to Him in prayer there was peace. Please pray for me that I will not close my heart to God's will and be consumed by worry and fear. Help me to walk each moment, one at a time, with Jesus and truly desire only His will. Please pray for Michael that God will heal him. Thank you, Jacob. I know you understand all things and see as God sees. Please help us keep our eyes set on Jesus. You know what is ultimately most important. Please pray for all of us accordingly. I love you, Jacob-my baby, and now my beautiful, holy Saint of God!

September 26, 2001

Dear Jacob,

Why do I waste so much of my life worrying? I did it all through my pregnancy with you. Now I am doing it with Michael's headache. I feel emotionally drained, out of sorts, overwhelmed, stressed out, etc. I haven't kept up on my duties around the house. I haven't given the kids much affection and attention. I feel no peace of body, mind, soul, or spirit. Please pray for me. Pray that I will learn to live _every_ moment to the fullest and accept _everything_ as God's will. Pray that I will quit wasting my time and energy on worrying.

Jesus, please help me. Conform my will to Yours and help me to be faithful to You always. Show us the depth of Your love and help us to open our hearts to Your will and also experience the love and joy that You desire for all people. Help Chris and me and all of us to see that each moment of each day is part of Your plan for us and that it is a glorious and beautiful plan. Please forgive me for all the time I have wasted in worry. Please help me to relax and find peace even in the midst of chaos and seeming darkness. I love You, Lord. I love you, Jacob. Pray for all of us.

December 21, 2001
(Today is your feast day)

My dearest Jacob,

One year ago today you entered Heaven with Jesus and all the Heavenly Hosts. I think back on all the happenings of that day, and I feel very sad. Yet when I went to Mass, I knew you were present with me in a much deeper way than you would have been if you had lived. My emotions can be so confusing. There is sadness, yet joy... emptiness, yet fullness... Then Father said the word, "mystery," and it struck me, for the word mystery describes it all perfectly. It is the mystery of eternity, and God's perfect plan and love for us and the Communion of Saints. I thank Jesus that He has allowed me to truly experience the Communion of Saints with you. Though I am sad this week and miss your bodily presence, I have peace and joy in my heart. For when I am with the Lord, especially in church, you are very very alive and present. Thank you for staying close to me. Please help me to always stay close to Jesus. I love you and always will.

This was the last time I wrote in Jacob's journal. As I look back on these journal entries, it is obvious how weak I am. Even though God showed me so clearly how beautiful His will is, I still struggle every single day to trust Him and let go of my own will. I was blessed to "see" a glimpse of Heaven, yet how quickly I forget and fight God's will. I do not in any way have it all figured out. I worry too much and trust too little. Right now, we all have to live in the human, physical world. Sometimes we have to suffer even when we can't see the beauty in it. God asks us to trust Him. No matter what we think or how we feel, we must strive always to surrender our own will and trust His. God's peace will rush in, and His grace will carry us through the storm. Trust that while He understands your pain and weeps with you, He also knows ultimately the beauty and goodness He has in store for you.

CALEB ISAAC ALFARO
July 25, 2002

About a year after Jacob died, around the time I finished journaling to him, we found out that I was pregnant again, and we were expecting our ninth baby.

January 27, 2002

My dearest new little one,

I am almost twelve weeks pregnant with you right now. Your due date is August 12th! I do not know if you are a girl or boy or what your name will be yet. But already I love you and desire you with all my heart. You have eight brothers and sisters - six brothers and two sisters. Being pregnant brings me great joy but also great fear. Three of your brothers and one of your sisters have died as infants. You see, our family has a genetic kidney disease that each of you children has a chance of developing while you are forming inside my womb. And I already fear for your life. I know that God created you perfect just as you are, and I know that God has a perfect plan for your life, whether it be long or short. I pray that I will have the grace to accept God's will for you, and that I can be totally conformed to God's will. That is the only way any of us will find peace and joy. But I just want you to know that I desire to have you here with me and to be able to mother you and love you on this earth. I want you so much, that it seems almost impossible to think about the possibility of you having the same kidney disease and the possibility of you dying. I want so badly to hold you and love you and kiss you and care

- 79 -

for you as your mommy. But... we must follow God's plans for our lives and He will care for us through it all. Just know, that <u>no matter what</u>, I love you with all my heart, and I <u>always</u> will.   Love, Mommy

I wrote only one time in my journal during this pregnancy. I knew very well all that God had done for me with and through Jacob, but I did not want to do it again. Truthfully, I struggled to even pray during this pregnancy, because when I prayed during my pregnancy with Jacob, God gave me a sense that he was sick. So this time I didn't even want to give God that chance. I was afraid of what God might ask of me. It is sad and embarrassing, that even though God filled me with a deeper joy than anything I had ever experienced, I still tried to take back control rather than fully trusting Him. I was and still am so weak, so human, so afraid. Jesus says in Matthew 8:26 "Why are you so terrified, O you of little faith?" Prayer and trust are what would have brought me peace and joy, rather than fear.

Beside the emotional struggle, this pregnancy was also a little more difficult physically than the others. I didn't have much energy at all, which made it tough trying to keep up with my four other children: Michael (12), Andrea (8), Seth (6), and Ethan (3). Thankfully, I didn't get sick, just very, very fatigued. This pregnancy was difficult, both physically and emotionally.

We found out by ultrasound we were having another boy, our seventh son and fifth boy in a row since our daughter Andrea had been born. We decided to name him Caleb Isaac. As Abraham was asked to give his son, Isaac, back to God, it had become a reality for us, that we had to be ready and willing to give our baby back to God each and every time we were expecting.

At the dreaded twenty-eight-week ultrasound, we were given the great news that Caleb's kidneys were perfectly healthy. Even with this assurance, as my due date drew closer, I was filled with anxiety and fear about losing him in labor. Emotionally, I was very weak. I couldn't relax. I felt like I just couldn't do this again.

As with almost all of my deliveries, Caleb came a few weeks early. That turned out to be a huge blessing in this case. When the placenta was delivered after Caleb had been born, the doctors discovered that part of the placenta was already dead tissue. The tissue had been dying before Caleb was even born. Eventually, it would not have supported his life any longer. This apparently is a condition that can happen in some women. The doctors said if it happens once, it is likely to happen more than once. Because of that, they concluded this must have been the reason Trini had died. I was, am, and always will be so thankful to God for sparing Caleb's life and helping him be born safe and healthy before the same thing could happen to him.

Caleb's birth and life brought us great joy. He was a very quiet, sweet, shy, and timid baby and toddler until he hit three years old. What I thought was a three-year-old phase turned out to be Caleb's more vibrant and passionate personality. Caleb is a perfectionist and competitor in everything he does. He feels every emotion very deeply and also thinks about everything very deeply. As a child, he has had a depth and spirituality far beyond his years.

MARY KATHERINE ALFARO

January 31, 2004

Before Caleb was even a year old, to our surprise I was pregnant again, with our tenth child. God was really teaching me I am not in control. After all we had been through, I realize I must be a very slow learner. At this point in my life, I was happy. My heart was full. I didn't want to go through another pregnancy. I didn't think I could possibly manage my five children and a pregnancy like Caleb's. I didn't have time to be super fatigued. I didn't want to go through it all again. I woke up a few nights in a row panicking that I just couldn't do it. After all my blessings, I am humbled and ashamed to admit how selfish I still was, thinking about myself and what I thought I wanted instead of the incredible gift and blessing of a new life.

We very quickly adapted to the idea of having another baby. To my delight, I was not fatigued at all during this pregnancy. I had plenty of energy for my kids, and it actually was a very easy and good pregnancy. Why do I continually doubt God? He knows what I need and always provides it. I had a sense very early on that this baby was a girl, and I was right. After five boys in a row, we were so excited to be having another little girl. Andrea's prayers were finally answered; she had waited ten long years for this! We named this baby Mary Katherine and planned to call her Mary-Kate.

Much like my pregnancy with Jacob, I had a sense that Mary-Kate might be sick, and that God may ask me to give her back. It wasn't super strong, but it was there. I wasn't sure if it was just my fear, or disbelief that I could actually have two healthy babies in a row. With the previous nine babies, that had only happened once before, with Andrea and Seth. About a month before my twenty-eight-week ultrasound, I went on retreat with my mom. While there, I wrote one of my first entries in Mary-Kate's journal:

October 25, 2003
(twenty-three weeks pregnant)

Dear Mary-Kate,

I am on retreat right now and missing all your brothers and your sister very much, but am so happy to have you with me. You are in my womb, and every movement I feel fills my heart with great joy and gratitude for you. I am so proud to have you, my 10th child, my third daughter. I am proud to finally know your name and write it down and write to you for the first time. You are moving within me as I write.

Mary-Kate, I do not know what the future holds for us, but Jesus does. He knows full well the plans He has in store for you. Plans for your welfare, not for woe. You are in His hands and in my heart. We, your family, pray for your health constantly. We await your birth and pray God will allow you to stay here on earth and grow with us. We thank God for you and long to keep you near to us, but we trust in God's plan for all of us. It is perfect. I love you, my sweet baby girl, Mary-Kate. Thank you for being with me now. You are precious. You are God's work of art, a miracle, His masterpiece. I love you...forever!

Once again while on retreat, I asked the priest if I could receive the Sacrament of the Sick for Mary-Kate and the genetic kidney condition. That Saturday night I received the Sacrament, just as I had six years earlier with John David. This time, as I was anointed, my mom heard the Lord say, "She will be fine." I call Mary-Kate my miracle baby. I will never know until I get to Heaven if Mary-Kate had the disease and was healed that day, but I do know that she was born beautifully healthy and had an overabundance of amniotic fluid. There was absolutely no question about the functioning of her kidneys.

I was overwhelmed by the gift of Mary-Kate's life. In fact, I was ashamed and humbled. I did not deserve such a gift. I had been so selfish. I needed to work through a lot of guilt about my confusing emotions when I first found out I was pregnant, and was so humbled by and grateful for the wisdom of the Catholic Church in giving us natural family planning (NFP). I am thankful that with NFP God is still in control. He knows what is best, not me. I didn't think I could handle another pregnancy right then, but He knew. I am thankful for the wisdom and guidance of the Church in our family: being fickle, fearful, and selfish, on my own I may have missed the beautiful gift of Mary-Kate. I was instantly in love with her. I was so humbled and grateful for God's perfect plan that I practically cried every night when I put her to bed for the first two years of her life. I am so blessed by her life. I cannot for one second imagine life without her.

Mary-Kate brought a radiant new spark to our family. She idolized her older sister and would do anything for her. At the same time, she had a spunk and sassiness that could challenge even the oldest of our boys. She could definitely hold her own around them. She had an independent and confident personality and liked to be in control. My mom once joked that I could just go take a nap because Mary-Kate had everything under control. Mary-Kate was the perfect addition to our wild and crazy boy-filled home.

PETER CHRISTOPHER ALFARO
July 6, 2007

At the age of thirty-nine, I became pregnant once again. This time there was a bigger space between pregnancies, so emotionally I think I was a little more prepared to handle another pregnancy and what it would mean for us. We had never had three healthy babies in a row, so we got back on that emotional rollercoaster, hoping God would spare the life of our eleventh child. Around twenty weeks into the pregnancy, we found out we were having another boy, our eighth. Our once-quiet home was very far from quiet and peaceful, but we love our boys. We named this son Peter Christopher and hoped and prayed for his health as he continued to develop.

At the dreaded twenty-eight-week ultrasound, we received the beautiful news that Peter's kidneys looked perfectly healthy. We began then to actually get excited and prepare for another baby. God is so good and blessed us with three healthy babies in a row. Maybe the genetic condition was actually healed when I was anointed with the Sacrament of the Sick while I was pregnant with Mary-Kate. We did not know, but either way we felt extremely blessed that Peter did not have ARPKD.

Very early in the morning on July 6, 2007, I was startled awake by a super hard kick or punch that broke my water. Labor got going pretty quickly after that; however, after several hours of labor, my uterus just kind-of quit and labor failed to progress. I ended up delivering Peter by C-section. After eleven babies in eighteen years, I think my uterus was done. The doctor said that when he got in there for surgery, the wall of my uterus was so thin it basically fell open. After that, my doctor told us it would be extremely dangerous for me to have another baby, that the baby and I could even die if the uterus were to rupture during pregnancy.

Being my eleventh delivery, I lost a lot of blood during surgery. I became extremely anemic and very very sick. I was faint and nauseated. Just sitting up made me ill. I didn't know how I could possibly go home and care for six children and a newborn baby. My parents offered to take care of us, and our whole family moved into their condo. Chris went back and forth to work from there while my mom and dad fed us and took care of all the kids when Chris was working. My mom and sister basically took care of little baby Peter around the clock for me. Pretty much all I was able to do was nurse him and then hand him back. I was so anemic that often just sitting up to nurse him would give me a headache. We stayed with my parents for about a month while I recovered.

It's funny how, when you look back on difficult times, you realize they were actually times of grace and blessing. Having that month with my parents ended up being one of those times. Little did we know that a year and a half later my mom would pass away from lung cancer. That month was a special time for her to be able to care for us, rather than having to be cared for. It was also time for her to build a special and close bond with her little Peter. In fact, some of her very last words before she died were, "What am I going to do without my little Peter?" And that month was also very special for me to once more be taken care of by my mom. I will always treasure that gift.

Despite the difficult delivery, Peter has been an absolute joy every single day of his life. He is a bouncy and imaginative little boy. He continues to bring a purity and childlike innocence to our family, as many of our older children are becoming adults. Nine years old now, I told him just the other night, that even when he is over six feet tall, he will still be my little Peter.

PRAYERS ANSWERED

God has given me a wonderful husband and 11 babies in 18 years of childbearing, which has resulted in 27 years of parenting so far--with many more to come. Through my experiences with grief, He has given me a glimpse of Heaven and allowed me to see in a very real way how perfect His plan is. When I embraced His holy darkness, instead of fighting it, I felt closer to God than ever. When I look back on those times, I realize they were some of the most beautiful and grace-filled times in my life. Yet, what do I do with it? If you can believe it, I still worry about every detail of my life and fight His will constantly. Ann Voskamp, a New York Times bestselling author, writes:

> Why do I lunge for control instead of joy? ...If I am rejecting the joy that is hidden somewhere deep in this moment, am I not ultimately rejecting God? Whenever I am blind to joy's well, isn't it because I don't believe in God's care? That God cares enough about me always to offer me joy's water, wherever I am, regardless of circumstance. But if I don't believe God cares, if I don't want or seek the joy he definitely offers somewhere in this moment-I don't want God. In His presence is fullness of joy. He is in this moment. The well is always here. God is always here-precisely because He does care (*One Thousand Gifts*, 130-131).

In January of 2016, I read this during my daily prayer: "Maturity in faith means the willingness to give up to the Lord everything that He gives us, and totally entrusting ourselves to him" (Fr. Tadeusz Dajczeren, *The Magnificat*, Jan. 2016). I am obviously pretty weak in faith as I continually seek control and fight surrender, even after all God has done for me. I have seen (a glimpse) and still struggle. Blest are you who have not seen and yet believe.

I most certainly do not have all the answers, but I can guarantee you that God loves you and His plan *is* perfect. It doesn't humanly make sense. When I look back on what happened to me, it seems unfathomable and unreal, but I can honestly tell you it was as real as anything physical I have ever seen or touched. It was supernatural and truly beautiful in every way. When I read over my journal, it reminds me and calls me back to that place of total surrender and trust. I realize that God answered my desperate prayer for Him to "show [His] love to me and bring me back to life again--even more vibrant and alive than before."

I hope that by sharing my experience, I can help encourage you to give God your pain and trust Him in *everything*. He is with you always and desires to delight your heart in His will. As Father Jim once told me, and I now truly understand, "We propose, but God alone disposes and will delight us in it." For it says in Scripture: "I have come that they might have life, and have it to the full" (John 10:10). With God, there is joy, even in the cross. The single greatest and deepest joy I have ever had in my life came in the cross.

When I think of all of my children and my ultimate desire for each of them, it is that they may have the gift of eternal life. This life is a gift, but our true home is in Heaven with Jesus. Four of my eleven children have already reached their ultimate goal. While their lives seemed way too short, it is a gift to know that they are safely home. The rest of us are still on the journey, fighting for our lives as we try to fulfill God's purpose for us. We have much work to do. Trini, Nicole, Jack, and Jacob have reached their goal and won the crown. They are now alive in the presence of Jesus in perfect joy. Now in God's presence they intercede for us every single day. Father Jim once said that not a day would go by that they did not mention our names to Jesus. We are truly blessed by their lives.

For each of my living children, grandchildren, and future grandchildren, I pray they will recognize that each and every day we are in a battle for our souls. I pray they will keep their eyes fixed on Jesus, fight the good fight, and never give up. Life will be hard and filled with struggles of all sorts. None of us, as hard as we may try, can escape that, but I know for a fact that Jesus is and always will be with them through it all. I pray they remember where their true joy is, that they surrender and open their hearts to Him. His plan is perfect, and as St. Augustine said, "their hearts will be restless, until they rest in Him."

As I said in the very beginning, my dream was to be a wife and mother. I didn't know all that would entail, but God allowed me to live that dream. I am truly blessed to have been given my dream, but what I have learned is that the only way our dreams will bring us true joy is if we surrender them completely to Christ. Sensing God's presence and personal love and care for us comes through surrender and submission to God. Whatever you are holding on to, whether it be a relationship, sorrow, suffering, fear, goals, or your hopes and dreams, trust in God's love for you and His plan for your life. If you keep Him first in your life, everything else will fall into place, and if you continually surrender yourself completely to His perfect plan, as a wise and holy priest once said to me, "He *will* delight you in it!"

EPILOGUE
April 2017

Here I am, sixteen years after having lost Jacob, and I have finally written my story. At least I thought I was finished, but God had other plans...

SETH THOMAS ALFARO
February 13, 2017

Around seven pm on the night of February 13, 2017, I heard a frantic knock on our door. I opened it to find a police officer who informed us that our twenty-one-year-old son, Seth, had been in a horrible accident, falling twenty-five feet through a roof onto concrete. No words can describe our feelings of horror in that moment.

After a police escort to the hospital, we were ushered into a small private room in the emergency room waiting area and told that they would be sending in a social worker to talk to us. A social worker was coming to talk to us? I thought he must be dead. They must have been getting the social worker to tell us Seth was dead. Instead of the social worker, however, the trauma doctor who had been working on Seth came in to talk to us. He told us that Seth had bleeding in his brain. I asked him if Seth could die from this. He replied, "Yes, he could."

That night, our lives changed in an instant. We found ourselves back in the ICU, but this time at the bedside of our lifeless twenty-one-year-old son. Seth was totally unresponsive and in an induced coma. We were in shock. I literally felt sick to my stomach and thought I was going to throw up. I was not ready to surrender my child to Christ yet again. Not now. Not like this. This couldn't be happening...

The words in this book ran through my head. I had been working on it all year. I was just about finished writing it. I knew that true joy was in God's will, but how could this possibly be it? How could I possibly surrender Seth? Seth was full of life! He had big dreams. In fact, just the night before, Chris and I had had a conversation with Seth about his hopes and dreams. We told him that no matter what he achieves in life, he will never be truly happy unless he is in God's will. This was definitely not what I was thinking when I said that. Those words played over and over in my mind. I said them. I believed them. And now, somehow, I would have to live them...

I didn't know how, after twenty-one years, I could possibly surrender Seth to Christ. I don't know if I ever truly did, but I tried, and that is what God asks of us. I had to make a conscious act of the will to surrender, no matter how I felt.

On February 19th, six days after Seth's accident, he was still in a coma with more complications arising. Chris and I were fighting serious discouragement. We felt as if our faith knees were buckling. We couldn't take it any longer. Both of us left Seth's hospital room and went our separate ways to try to collect ourselves. Chris went for a walk outside and his solace came through the Rosary. I went to the hospital Chapel to cry and pray. What was God doing? I cried and cried and cried. I just couldn't surrender Seth. "Please, Lord, no," I begged. I wrestled with God. I wrestled with myself. I knew I had to surrender Seth to God. I knew that somehow God's plan was best, but I couldn't see it. I couldn't understand it, and I just didn't want it to be this way. I knelt there in that chapel sobbing and talking out loud to God. I was doubled over, clenching my fists, pleading with God. I knew I had to end my prayer with those words, "Your will, not mine, be done." I couldn't do it. I didn't understand it. I fought it... but finally, with tears streaming down my cheeks, and clenched teeth, I uttered those words, "Your will, Lord, not mine, be done for Seth." There was no sentiment or warm fuzzy feeling. It was purely a heart-wrenching, conscious act of my will. And from there I had to continue to pray constantly for the grace to surrender every single day and trust God's will for Seth's life. Thankfully, there were hundreds, probably even thousands, of people praying for Chris and I and our family and all the graces we needed to walk this harrowing path.

Once again, a prayer of mine from many years earlier had been answered. I had written to Jacob, "Pray that we all continue to grow closer to Jesus and that my will be conformed to God's will in the little things, shocking things, and even huge tragedies-- everything." Be careful what you pray for.

I have been humbled once again. At a time when I doubted God the most, He was answering the deepest prayer and longing of my heart for Seth: that he know, love, and serve God with all his heart. God has once again given me a glimpse of Heaven. This time, through the eyes and heart of my twenty-one-year-old son. I don't know why God has given me so many gifts. They are not mine to just hold onto. I believe they are given to share. So, God willing, I will write another book to share our family's journey through Seth's traumatic brain injury and miraculous recovery. I pray that through my stories, God will touch your hearts in whatever way He desires.

I do not have all the answers. I struggle every single day to surrender my will and trust God, just like everyone else. God, however, has shown me time and time again that His will is bigger than mine and more beautiful than I can imagine. God tells us in Isaiah 55:8-9, "For my thoughts are not your thoughts, neither are your ways my ways ... As the heavens are higher than the earth, so are my ways higher than your ways and my thoughts than your thoughts." Surrendering to His will is the key to peace and joy. No matter what you are going through, hold tight to Christ!

This life is often a valley of tears, but our reward will be great in Heaven. And Heaven must be absolutely amazing beyond all telling if a twenty-one-year-old young man, full of hopes, dreams, and passion, is lying in a hospital bed unable to walk, eat, or care for himself, barely able to talk, and still declares, "This is a blessing. The gifts God gives are greater than anything else we could ever imagine."

I do believe that God's will, whether I understand it at the time or not, truly is the delight of my heart.

About the Author

Christine Alfaro was born and raised in Rockford, Michigan. At nineteen years old, she met her husband, Christopher, while attending Franciscan University of Steubenville in Ohio. They got married on December 17th, 1988 and just recently celebrated their 30th anniversary. Together they have eleven children ranging in age from eleven to twenty-nine, and four grandchildren. Christine and her family currently reside in Grand Rapids, Michigan.

After her son's tragic accident and miraculous recovery in 2017, she was invited to speak and share her story at her home parish. Since then, she has also spoken at numerous other events in multiple states. She is working on growing her ministry while also supporting the growth of her son's ministry– Seth Alfaro Ministries. It is her strong belief that these experiences are not just meant for them, but to be shared with others.

To contact or book Christine, email her at
chrsitinealfaro1028@gmail.com

To learn more about Seth's story and ministry visit
www.sethalfaroministies.com

28599270R00055

Made in the USA
Lexington, KY
20 January 2019